EVASIONS
The American Way
of Military Service

EVASIONS
The American Way
of Military Service

Philip Gold

PARAGON HOUSE PUBLISHERS

New York

Published in the United States by
Paragon House Publishers
2 Hammarskjold Plaza
New York, New York 10017

Designed by Marcy Katz Schusterman

Library of Congress Cataloging-in-Publication Data

Gold, Philip, 1948–
    Evasions: The American Way of Military Service.

    Bibliography:
    Includes index.
    1. Military service, Compulsory—United States.
2. Duty. I. Title.
UB343.G63   1985   355.2′2363′0973   85–19171
ISBN 0–913729–05–1

First printing, February 1986.

CONTENTS

FOREWORD

Most of today's rhetoric on the reform of America's defenses centers on numbers—numbers of nuclear warheads, of intercontinental missiles, of ships, of planes, of tanks, of guns. Most of all it centers on the numbers of our tax dollars spent on all this hardware. While numbers are important, they are secondary to the most important question of all: will Americans risk, and if necessary sacrifice, their very lives to man these weapon systems? If that question cannot be satisfactorily answered, all the numbers are meaningless and even the most expensive weapon systems just so much worthless junk.

Contrary to what you might believe, the answer is not evident. Indeed, it has never been evident. We remember the heroic tales of Andrew Jackson rallying the good people of New Orleans to turn back the British invasion there, and conveniently forget that after the burning of the White House earlier in that war a British naval force sailed up the Potomac to menace Alexandria, and when the valiant soldiers of the Virginia militia came galloping to the rescue a citizen's commission met them outside the town and told them to bug off. They had already struck a bargain with the invaders and didn't want to risk having their homes destroyed by a British bombardment. And this is not just ancient history. In 1985, a group of American citizens, also concerned at putting themselves at risk, attempted to force a referendum to bar the *USS Iowa* from establishing a home port in the New York City harbor. A common defense is all well and good, they seemed to be saying, but providing for it is some one else's responsibility.

As the war in Vietnam illustrated, this mind set can have tragic consequences. Because the "whiz kids" in the Pentagon saw war only in quantifiable terms—number of ships, guns, planes, missiles; the body count of enemy soldiers killed; the statistics on numbers of villages pacified—they completely ignored the moral dimension of that struggle. President Lyndon Johnson, fearful of stirring up the passions of the American people in support of the war lest it jeopardize his Great Society programs, was only too happy with this omission. And academic theorists also played a part. Becoming the American version of the "vanguard of the proletariat" who knew what was best for the American people, their limited war theories totally ignored the role of the public in strategy formulation. The result was that we tried to fight the war in "cold blood." Our failure was eminently predictable.

One of the positive results of that war is that within the military there has been a return to fundamentals, especially a return to the fundamentals of military theory. A century and a half ago, Karl von Clausewitz, drawing on his experience in the Napoleonic Wars, discovered what he called the "remarkable trinity" of the government, the army, and the people. It is the government that sets the direction of war and in so doing sets the objectives which determine the value of the struggle.

It is the army (what today we would call the armed forces) that is the instrument of war. But it is the passions of the people that are the very engine of war. They are the ones who pay the price. It is their sons and daughters who fill the ranks, it is their moneys that buy the arms and equipment, and it is their will and determination that enables the nation to stay the course.

Georgetown Professor Philip Gold, in this masterful treatise on American military service, has also returned to fundamentals. As he makes clear, Clausewitzian theory is only a reaffirmation of the lessons learned by our Founding Fathers 50 years before Clausewitz's *On War* was written, lessons incorporated into our very Constitution. As Professor Gold emphasizes, it is this concept of "civic virtue," not arms and equipment, that is the true basis of America's national security. Military reform must begin with an appreciation of this fundamental truth, and *Evasions: The American Way of Military Service* provides the means to do just that.

> Colonel Harry G. Summers, Jr., now Senior Military Correspondent for *US News and World Report,* formerly held the General Douglas MacArthur Chair of Military Research at the Army War College. He is the author of *On Strategy* and the *Vietnam War Almanac.*

PREFACE

Some one, either Mark Twain or Winston Churchill (or maybe both), once remarked that there are "lies, damned lies, and statistics." Whoever it was, he might usefully have added that nowhere are the lies and statistics more damnable than at those volatile human frontiers where hard realities and transcendent purposes collide.

In December 1981, I received a grant for research and writing on the question of military service in America. As originally conceived, the project would have generated a "Why-We-Need-the-Draft-Back" monograph, concentrating on the military and narrowly political aspects of the question. But as I researched and wrote some preliminary columns and articles, it became clear to me that neither the statistics (grim though they are) nor the standard arguments favoring citizen military service (valid though they might be) could justify any return to peacetime conscription. It is not so much that these arguments (and their supporting statistics) are wrong, as that they fail to address the historically unprecedented condition of contemporary American society, and the equally unprecedented dangers which confront that society. A new approach is needed, one that melds traditional (and still valid) insights with military and political realities unimaginable only a few years ago. This book is an attempt at such an approach.

Parts of this book originally appeared as essays in *The Public Interest* and *The Washington Quarterly*. Permission to reprint parts of those essays is gratefully acknowledged for:

> *The Public Interest*, "What the Reserves Can—and Can't —Do," Spring 1984.
> *The Washington Quarterly*, "Military Service in America," Summer 1983, MIT Press.

Permission to quote from the following works is also gratefully acknowledged:

> John Lewis Gaddis, *Strategies of Containment*, Oxford University Press, 1982.
> George Kennan, "The Sources of Soviet Conduct," *Foreign Affairs*, July 1947. Copyright 1947 by The Council on Foreign Relations, Inc.
> Andy Mager, "I Won't Register for the Draft," *New York Times*, January 5, 1985.

While engaged in this project, I've been fortunate to receive support, criticism, guidance, and the insights of the following: Joe Harper, Roger Kaplan, Les Lenkowsky, Mack Owens, Jeff Record, R. Randolph Richardson, and Admiral Jim Stockdale. Thanks to you all. Thanks also to the folks at Paragon House for an exceptionally pleasant publishing experience. Thanks also to my students in History 236, "War and U.S. Society," for hard questions, high interest, and a good bit of fun.

INTRODUCTION

The society that draws a line between its fighting men and its thinking men will find its fighting done by fools and its thinking done by cowards.

Sir William Francis Butler

On April 9, 1985, an article headlined, "Enlistment Decline Brings Call for New Draft," appeared on page one of the *New York Times*. The article, written by the *Times'* respected military correspondent Richard Halloran, noted that "young men and women have become less interested in enlisting in the armed forces," that enlistments have fallen off "slightly," and that "these signs have made advocates of volunteer armed services nervous."

That article should have been headlined, "A Crisis Lies Ahead"—a crisis which may or may not coincide with a war, and which may even coincide with some relaxation of international tension, but which lies ahead nonetheless. The nature of this crisis is relatively easy to state. By the end of this decade (if not already), the United States of America will no longer be able to generate military manpower sufficient to meet its commitments, defend its economic interests, or even to guarantee continued access to large portions of the planet.

Or, to put it another way:

Absent fundamental changes in the way America presently raises and supports its armed forces, or unilateral strategic disengagement from most of the non-Marxist world, the United States will find itself, for all practical purposes, militarily impotent.

The confluence of circumstances and forces creating this crisis is also relatively easy to define. Four sets of factors are responsible.

First, American military commitments *since Vietnam* have undergone a quantum expansion, due both to inexorably increasing Soviet military power and to the escalating chaos in regions whose security once required only marginal American attention. Today, the United States plans for combat literally everywhere on earth: not only in the traditional theaters of Central Europe and Northeast Asia, but also in the newer danger zones of the Middle East and Southwest Asia, and in a

Western Hemisphere whose continued non-Marxist character can no longer be taken for granted. Add to this residual commitments in Southeast Asia, and a plethora of other guarantees and undertakings, and the dilemma becomes clear.

No nation in history has ever attempted to fulfill such an array of military obligations. Nor has any ever attempted to fulfill them by relying entirely on citizen volunteer forces.

The second factor is changing demography. According to Census Bureau statistics reported in Mr. Halloran's article, the military-age cohort—the pool of eighteen-to-twenty-one year-old men and women from which recruits are normally drawn—will drop from 15.4 million in 1985 to 13 million in 1995. These figures actually understate the problem, for they include both men and women, the college-bound and high school dropouts, the fit and unfit. In reality, only a small percentage of the total pool is both interested in and qualified for military service: a percentage which invariably shrinks even more in times of prosperity. But whatever the percentage, the trend is clear. The last of the baby boom generation has passed military age, and for the rest of this century America's military will have to be recruited from a diminishing manpower pool.

And this at a time when America's military commitments have reached historically unprecedented levels.

The third factor is the peculiar nature of the Reagan rearmament program. By opting to invest heavily in hardware while eschewing any significant increase in uniformed end strength, by opting, in effect, to ignore the problem, the Reagan administration has only postponed the day of reckoning. At some point (if not already), hundreds of thousands of additional personnel will be needed to sail those new ships, fly and maintain those new aircraft, operate those new weapons systems, fill out those new divisions. Granted, much can be done to alleviate the shortfall by liberalizing entry standards, increasing recruitment of women, admitting so-called undocumented aliens to service, offering greater re-enlistment incentives, using personnel more efficiently, etc. But none of these palliatives, nor all of them together, will resolve the basic problem of how to raise and support a standing force capable of fighting almost anywhere on short-to-no-notice. At present, the United States maintains an active force of about 2.15 million men and women. In order to maintain this end strength, between 200,000 and 300,000 new recruits must enter the services annually. By some estimates, 300,000 young men and women will constitute almost the entire interested-and-qualified pool in 1995.

And this at a time when hundreds of thousands of additional personnel will be required, if the Reagan administration's multi-trillion dollar expenditures are not to purchase weapons with no one to use them.

The fourth and final factor is the changing nature of the continuum of violence which America must face, if America desires to remain the ultimate guarantor of such freedom as still exists (or may potentially exist) in the world. An unprecedented array of perils now confront us: from the Soviet buildup (the greatest peacetime armaments program in human history) and an increasing Soviet willingness to use those arms, to the newer problems of Soviet surrogates such as Cuba and Nicaragua, to the assorted barbarities of resurgent Islamic fundamentalism. Once upon a time, not so very long ago, the United States could tailor its conventional forces to the special requirements of European war, while assuming that "minor" conflicts (such as Vietnam) need not consume its military substance. Once upon a time, not so very long ago, Iranian deserts and Salvadoran hills figured primarily in command-and-staff college academic exercises. And, once upon a time, not so very long ago, the United States could count on technological superiority, an inviolable homeland, and allies and surrogates who would do most of the dying until the country got its act together and took it on the road.

No more. And, in all probability, never again.

But if the nature of the problem seems clear, the answers do not. Proposed solutions vary wildly, from neo-isolationism to universal military service. Interestingly, the authors of these various proposals defy neat political categorization. Among the proponents of full or partial American military withdrawal from Europe, for example: left-libertarian Earl Ravenal, Democratic Senator and defense expert Sam Nunn, military reformer Jeffrey Record, and neo-conservative journalist Irving Kristol. Among the proponents of revived conscription: *Atlantic Monthly* editor (and self-confessed draft evader) James Fallows, neo-conservative *Commentary* editor Norman Podhoretz, Democratic Senator Ernest Hollings, and former Democratic presidential candidate Gary Hart (who favors universal national service with civilian and military options). And, perhaps most remarkable of all, a significant segment of the nuclear pacifist movement now argues for increases in conventional armament as an alternative to theater and tactical nuclear weapons—an advocacy which usually ignores the question of where the troops are coming from. But none of these positions, whatever their partial truths, offers a comprehensive solution to America's present dilemma and impending crisis. None of them addresses the problem in its entirety. For all evade the quintessential question, which must be posed explicitly, and then explicitly answered, before any of the strategic, military, and political vexations can be faced. This essential question is, simply:

Does citizen military service any longer rationally relate either to the obligations of citizenship in a mature mass democracy such as America, or to the realities of the kinds of wars America is likely to fight?

Or, to ask it in triune form:

First, can military service still be counted among the obligations of citizenship in a civilization where citizenship seems
reduced to the acceptance of benefits and the exercise of
dissent, and where the very concept of obligation — of
civic virtue—seems to have lost all meaning? Or might it be
more reasonable to deal in what Eliot Cohen has called "intermediate levels of obligation"—the idea that the citizen
may owe military service for certain contingencies (such as
home defense), but not for others? Whatever the specifics,
this is primarily a question of political and moral philosophy
and must be settled prior to any discussion of military strategies and needs. If a military obligation, even an "intermediate" obligation, exists, then it may be adapted to real-
world needs in many ways. If no citizen obligation exists,
then issues of strategy and policy became academic, and
the United States had better adjust its international behavior accordingly.

Second, if an obligation to serve does exist, what present
and future purposes might it serve? This is primarily a
question of national grand strategy. What does the United
States wish to accomplish in this world? What does it wish
to prevent? America has spent this century as a world
power with ever-increasing commitments. But today,
America's alliances and commitments do not contribute to
our physical security. In fact, they endanger it. A United
States whose interests and activities did not extend beyond
America would have very little to fear from the Russians, or
anybody else. All that would be necessary to ensure America's physical survival would be the maintenance of some
minimal nuclear deterrent, plus a willingness to deal with a
Marxist planet on whatever terms the Marxists might care
to make available. In order to protect our physical survival,
America does not need armies piled on armies, or trillion
dollar defense budgets. Nor does America need citizen military service, conscripted or voluntary. It is only when our
purpose as a nation extends beyond our own physical survival that the issue of citizen military obligation arises at all.
Nobody is about to invade America. We literally do not
have to defend ourselves in the traditional manner of repelling a cross-border attack. We face no significant cross-bor-

der terrorist threat, either. For what purposes, then, do we require over two million of our citizens in uniform? This question of purpose, of grand strategy, must be answered coherently, without recourse to the stale rhetorics of patriotism and sacrifice, if the concept of citizen obligation is to make any sense in the world of the late twentieth century.

Third, if a citizen obligation exists, and if it is to be reified in support of coherent American grand strategy, what form shall it take? At issue here is not only the perennial voluntarism *versus* conscription debate, but also the reform of a military establishment which (Grenada notwithstanding) has known nothing but defeat for a generation. No citizenry, no matter how sure of its obligations, no matter how certain of the rightness of its nation's goals, can be expected to support a military establishment that has lost, or abdicated, its competence in the art of war. Today, the war-making competence of the American military remains questionable, regardless of the optimistic press releases or the magnitude of the budgets.

In sum, then, if the present dilemma and impending crisis are to be addressed in any comprehensive manner, discussion must include not only an honest assessment of the statistics and the present state of the military, but also a clear statement of American purpose on this planet, and the relationship of the citizenry to that purpose.

The primary purpose of this book is to attempt just that.

In order to do so, it will be necessary to work through three distinct but nonetheless inter-related sets of problems: philosophy, history, and public policy.

The first part of this book examines the philosophical bases of military claim and obligation as seen in the Western heritage of just (or justifiable) war, and the matter of individual conscience as it pertains to the bearing of arms. Any legitimate state claim to citizen military service, compulsory or otherwise, must at least accord with the spirit of the just war heritage; any conscientious refusal to bear arms must at least acknowledge it. For the just war heritage, far from mandating warfare *per se*, actually provides an organizing paradigm and a rudimentary working vocabulary by which and through which citizen and state may communicate on the subject. Indeed, the just war vocabulary provides the only commonality of meaning possible in a democratic, pluralistic society: a fact far from obvious in a civilization such as ours, conditioned to equate conscience with dissent, and the willingness to bear arms with moral abdication, mindless chauvinism, or worse.

Part II moves from philosophy to history, examining the American experience with just warfare and dissent in two case studies: the American Revolution and Vietnam. Why these two seemingly irreconcilable episodes? Because the Revolution and Vietnam, taken together, reveal what may be termed the essential American understanding of citizen military obligation and service, and reveal it in ways that our other conflicts do not. Histories of America's wars abound; histories of conscription and resistance also exist by the hundreds. None of these, however, demonstrate with sufficient clarity the essential continuity of the American understanding and the relevance of that understanding to the present moment.

The final part, policy, addresses the questions of national purpose and the military requirements generated thereby. It assesses the present cold reality: expanding commitments, shrinking resources, unprecedented hazards, a defense establishment of questionable competence, and an essentially sterile, now nearly-forty-years-old grand strategy. Finally, the book addresses conscription, the arguments for and against, and the possibility of a draft based upon the concept of "intermediate obligation."

In this volume, I offer no specific proposals, no partisan agenda, no clarion calls to universal service, no glorification of the military experience, no worship of sacrifice as the highest manifestation of patriotism. I do, however, wish to reaffirm the following:

That the prudent defense of the global structure of freedom, a defense which is not and cannot be solely, or even primarily military, is and ought to be the American purpose.

That while the state, acting as the agent of the citizenry, may legitimately claim the military services of any or all of its citizens, only the reasoned consent of the individual adds the moral dimension of obligation.

And that, should be prudent defense of the global structure of freedom necessitate the employment of military force, such employment could be just.

One
PHILOSOPHY

Foundations of the Military Claim: Just War

Just war must be made possible and only just war should be allowed as a possibility.

Paul Ramsey
War and the Christian Conscience

The military claim, as the term will be used here, means simply this: the legal demand which a democratic state, acting as
the agent of its citizenry, may make upon that citizenry (or
upon those aspiring to citizenship) for service under arms in
war and peace. A clear enough definition, it would seem, but
one that also requires a bit of explication. For the military
claim does not operate in an ethical, historical, or political vacuum. Nor are democracies infallible, least of all in their foreign
policies. Nor are citizens omniscient, least of all in their assessment of those policies. Therefore, neither the legitimate claim
of the state nor the inalienable conscience of the individual can
serve as sole and final arbiter in the matter, without the former either violating the individual or the latter rendering the
state unable to provide for the common defense. If state claim
and individual conscience are to have any coherent, comple-
mentary meaning, individual and state must speak to each
other, each in a language that the other can understand.

For a generation now, the military claim has been commonly viewed as the essentially amoral (or immoral) demand
which the state makes upon an indifferent, alienated, or antag-
onistic citizenry. Too often, this view has been buttressed by
two conclusions drawn from a circumstance of political life.
Since those most susceptible to the military claim, young
adults, rarely enjoy any significant influence over the making
of national policy, lack of direct participation somehow negates the claim's validity. From this conclusion often flows another: that, in the absence of direct participation, the proper
citizen response should be appeal to private (not to say idio-
syncratic) conscience, followed by rejection or evasion of the
claim in all its manifestations (such as draft registration). And,
too often, this pseudo-interaction has been portrayed as simply the clash of irreconcilable opposites, with the resisting or
evading individual cast in the role of hero-martyr, and the
state condemned to play the role of heartless, if not demonic,
oppressor.

This view is worse than simplistic. It is a luxury this civilization can no longer afford, and not only because it ignores the fact that ours is a representative, not a direct democracy. It also ignores the fact that, in matters relating to service and conscience, individual and state must talk to, not past each other. There must be a commonly understood moral nexus between the conscience of the individual and the conscience of the state, as that conscience is legally and constitutionally embodied. There must be a common, if minimal, working vocabulary, if individual and state are to address each other without recourse to the sterile confrontations of *raison d'état* versus *raisons du coeur.*

Such a vocabulary exists. Or, to be more precise, such a vocabulary is in process of revivification. Historically and philosophically, this vocabulary is known as the heritage of just (or justifiable) war: a body of thought and experience which holds that armed conflict, like all other human activities, must be judged according to standards of purpose and conduct, of right and wrong. The just war heritage is a complex, often obscure, and occasionally contradictory amalgam of theological, philosophical, legal, political, and military concepts and practices. It is a heritage well over two thousand years old, and still evolving. It is, for reasons to be explored in this and the next chapter, the *sole* basis upon which individual and state may communicate in the matter of military service, if the two wish to communicate in good faith, and be understood.

Or, as James Turner Johnson has written in his study, *Can Modern War Be Just?*: "These ideas represent . . . the only way actually open for persons in our culture to think about morality and war. . . . If one side of the dilemma before us is how to apply the moral wisdom contained in the just war tradition to the case of contemporary war, the other side is that we cannot escape doing so."[1]

The just war heritage, then, is far more than some philosophical tinker toy, designed for the amusement of pedants and obscurantists far removed from the battlefield. It is also more than a simple ethical checklist whose mechanical use guarantees either moral decision-making or prudent policy. Rather, the just war heritage provides a conceptual framework within which the individual must evaluate his or her responses to armed conflict, and then communicate those responses to the larger society, and to society's agent, the state. And the just war heritage also provides the conceptual framework by which society and state must justify any recourse to arms, and the standard by which that recourse must be judged.

THE LANGUAGE OF JUST WAR

For as long as there has been armed conflict between political entities, there have been attempts to impose categories of permissible and impermissible—of right and wrong—upon that conflict. As a product of Western civilization, these attempts constitute the just (or justifiable) war heritage: a tradition today more valuable for its basic insights, for what Johnson has called its "practical moral wisdom," than for its arcana or its more obsolescent provisos.[2] That states once fought, for example, to regain a king's wife hardly means that infidelity in high places should constitute a *casus belli* today. But that men and women have historically regarded certain issues and certain causes beyond their own physical survival as worth fighting for matters a great deal.

At the outset, however, it is vital to reaffirm that the modern just war heritage, that which has evolved since the seventeenth century, exists independently of, and emphatically rejects, both the pacifist and the crusading impulses. The former elevates an individual witness, or a personal preference, to the

level of an absolute, without regard for the earthly consequences to one's self, one's society, or one's world; all that
matters is a certain form of abstinence, a certain form of pu-
rity. In the Western tradition, such indiscriminate pacifism (as
opposed to selective pacifism, a far more complex phenomenon) derives largely from a certain stylized interpretation of
Christian writ—an interpretation which overlooks far more
than it acknowledges.[3]

Christ spoke to individuals, not governments. The kingdom
and the peace he declared were not of this world, and on matters of war and peace he had practically nothing to say (although the imagery of warfare permeates the Gospels). The
essential message of Christianity involves the salvation of
souls, not the formulation of state policy, and Christ (at least
to judge from the story of the centurion) did not deem military
service a significant barrier either to faith or to redemption.

Christianity, however, does mandate a certain attitude toward one's fellow human beings: an attitude of responsibility
and care. Clearly, the taking of human life can never be an intrinsic good, and a Christian who accepts for himself an undif-
ferentiated, universalized responsibility for others may choose
never to engage in war. Both scriptural exegesis and early tradition offer a certain minimal support for this stance, although
it might be noted that, within a few centuries after Christ, non-
violence had become a priestly, not a lay virtue.

But Christians, for the most part, don't live alone. They live
in polities, i.e., within complex lattice-works of obligation and
responsibility toward specific others: family, community, country. Properly understood and implemented, these secular responsibilities constitute an exercise in applied Christianity
every bit as valid as total individual pacifism, total individual
celibacy, or any other form of total abstinence from the affairs
and imperfections of this world. For nearly two millennia,
Christian doctrine has both reaffirmed the correctness of these

responsibilities and also cautioned against the idolatry of self: the quest for an individual perfection simply not available in civilized existence, or on earth. For nearly two millennia, also, Christian doctrine has suggested that, under certain circumstances, participation in warfare *as a means of protecting others* might not be inconsistent with Christian teaching. Indeed, according to Saint Augustine, the first Christian just war apologist, such participation could constitute a positive duty.[4]

In this sense, then, the just war heritage stands, not as a vindication of warfare *per se*, but as a warning (one of many in Christian thought) against any attempt to derive a political policy from a personal witness, and to elevate that policy to the level of a religious absolute. For to do so is, in the largest sense, idolatrous. And the just war heritage also rejects the notion that those individuals who choose indiscriminate, total pacifism as *their* form of witness have any right to demand that their polities do the same. For to do so is to endanger others whom the individual, no matter what his beliefs, has no right to hazard—for by his refusal to protect them, he has already endangered them enough. And by becoming one more non-defender in need of *their* protection, he has already burdened them enough.

By the same token, the just war heritage also rejects the crusading impulse: the notions that the ends justify the means, and that the ends so transcend the means that war and violence become merely incidental, or else positive goods. Just as, since the end of the Wars of Religion in the seventeenth century, this tradition has rightly rejected warfare on behalf of God, so it also rejects the idea that proponents of any political ideology can justify the unlimited use of force. The just war heritage correctly disavows both extremes, holding that neither indiscriminate pacifism nor limitless violence are appropriate. Just war doctrine, in short, suggests that the moral response to the fact of warfare is also the prudent, temperate, and limited one.

Or, as William V. O'Brien, a contemporary student of the subject, has put it: "Given the unacceptability of total war on the one hand, and the virtually nonexistent hopes for a world without war on the other, some kind of just and limited war remains a necessity."[5]

This formulation—just and limited—is crucial. By definition, just war *is* limited war, and the limitation of war in both purpose and intensity is the *sine qua non* of any attempt to deal with war (to borrow John Courtney Murray's evocative phrase) "on a minimal basis of reason."[6]

Clearly, then, neither crusading nor indiscriminate pacifism belongs to the modern heritage. Perhaps all that remains to be said of the crusader and the indiscriminate pacifist, for the moment, is that they place themselves (albeit in very different ways) outside of civilized existence: the former because of his limitless ability to violate civilization, the latter by his refusal to defend it.

Having so argued, it is now necessary to sketch the contours of the just war vocabulary. As already noted, this vocabulary provides neither a mechanistic set of moral prescriptions nor a foolproof decision-making checklist. It offers only a place to start, a means of determining what kinds of standards to apply to a violent, disordered, potentially apocalyptic world.

The just war heritage consists of two separate but related parts: that pertaining to the going to war (in Latin, the *jus ad bellum*), and that pertaining to the conduct of war itself (the *jus in bello*). The *jus in bello* will not be of major concern in this inquiry. However, it is important to comment briefly on both its substance and its erroneous use in debate on the subject of military service as a whole.

The *jus in bello* is, by far, the more firmly established part of the heritage.[7] It exists in international and American law as the Law of Armed Conflict, the various Geneva and Hague Conventions, United Nations enactments, and the U.S. Uniform Code of Military Justice. Violations of these laws are punishable under both international and American law; violators have in the past been punished by both international and American tribunals. But the issue here is not whether soldiers, or states, can commit criminal acts, or wage criminal wars. They can. They have. They will. Rather, what matters here is whether the bearing of arms *per se* can be considered inevitably and invariably criminal because such crimes *may* occur.

The answer is, no. In this sense, the *jus ad bellum* and the *jus in bello* don't "mix." The probability, indeed the near-inevitability of violations within war does not automatically make war itself either illegal or unjust. Conceivably, a war may end up unjust because of the magnitude of the violations it occasioned, but to argue that all war is thereby rendered criminal is to substitute speculation and prophecy for fact.

But why go to war in the first place?

Over the millenia, different societies have attempted to answer this question in different ways. The primitives had their visions and rituals, the Hebrews their Old Testament guidance, the ancients their oracles and fetial rites. More secularized classical thinkers pondered the question at length. "That war which is necessary is just," said Livy.[8] "The only excuse for going to war," wrote Cicero, "is that we may live in peace unharmed."[9] Wise maxims, both, although not terribly informative. Saint Augustine considered warfare acceptable only as a constabulary measure, undertaken *in extremis* to protect the lives of others; neither glory nor aggrandizement, reasons acceptable to Livy and Cicero, had any place in early Christian formulations.[10] Not until Saint Thomas Aquinas, however, do we find a definitive, if still rudimentary, statement of the basic components: the essential just war vocabulary.[11] According to Aquinas, war may be undertaken justly only when all of the following criteria are met:

1) There must be just cause, either self-defense or the redress of grievance. No cause, however, may be considered just until all remedial measures short of war have failed. Further, the nature of the grievance or threat must be adequate to warrant the resort to arms; one must not risk losing more than one could gain (a point to which we must return when discussing so-called nuclear pacifism). Thus, proportionality as well as grievance or danger determines just cause.

2) There must be right intention, i.e., honesty of purpose. Legitimate aims and purposes must not be used as camouflage for other, unjust ambitions, nor must the destruction caused exceed that necessary to accomplish the legitimate objective. Again, proportionality helps determine right intention.

3) Finally, there must be an authority competent to initiate war, or to respond to attack: an authority responsible for and (in democratic polities) to the society which must endure the consequences of that decision. In the Western tradition, *competence de guerre* rests in the sovereign nation-state. In an emerging Marxist and Third World tradition, it rests in various non-sovereign political entities allegedly struggling for freedom from oppression, racism, imperialism, etc. In the American tradition, power to declare war resides in the Congress, although the President, in his capacity as Commander-in-Chief, has traditionally enjoyed a certain discretionary power in the use of force short of war.

Thus the essential vocabulary of the *jus ad bellum*: just cause, right intent, competent authority, with proportionality and prudence suffusing all three. In theory, the formulation seems self-evident. In practice, it often proves damnably hard to apply. What constitutes competent authority in cases such as Grenada or Beirut . . . or Vietnam? What constitutes just cause in the Persian Gulf or El Salvador . . . or Vietnam? What constitutes right intent and proportionality in an age of nuclear weapons, napalm, and helicopter gunships? Obviously, good-faith answers to these questions can vary wildly. In equal measure, the *jus ad bellum* can be invoked to justify wildly divergent judgements, depending upon who invokes it, and for what political, moral, or philosophical reasons. But what matters here is not agreement. What matters is that those who disagree be able to communicate. So long as they can, the prospect of mutual comprehension, if not accord, exists.

However, as we have already noted, there are those who, by choice, cannot use this vocabulary: crusaders and indiscriminate pacifists who claim unlimited primacy for their respective reasonings. There are, however, also those who, while perhaps not denying the abstract validity of the heritage, decline to use it. Rather often, this refusal is based upon either or both of two objections:

1) Nuclear pacifism (as opposed to indiscriminate pacifism)— the notion that the mere existence of nuclear weapons renders the entire concept of just warfare obsolete, no matter what validity it held in the past.

2) Legalism—the notion that the *jus ad bellum* is coterminous with existing international law, and that what has not been, or cannot be, so codified has no further relevance.

To take these objections in turn:

Since the end of the Second World War (and certainly since the possibility of "nuclear winter" has become scientifically respectable), a variety of analysts and polemicists have argued that the undeniable destructive potential of nuclear weapons has rendered the entire _jus ad bellum_ obsolete. "[T]he mere existence of nuclear weapons," writes Jesuit priest and former Congressman Robert F. Drinan, ". . . makes the possibility of a 'just' war so remote that the Church could and should condemn [all] warfare as morally objectionable."[12] Another writer, James W. Douglass, goes so far as to conclude that the _jus ad bellum_, "which has always upheld the value of violence as a form of justice, now has the task of upholding the value of a just refusal of violence."[13] These arguments cannot be dismissed out of hand, inasmuch as they raise vital questions of proportionality and the prudential calculation of risk: questions traditionally central to the heritage. But the analysts and polemicists err, for what they are saying is that the most minute possibility of nuclear warfare must always and forever be deemed an unacceptable risk. And since that possibility can usually be found in any confrontation (call it the Sarajevo Syndrome), all warfare automatically becomes unjust.

The problem with this argument is twofold. First, it substitutes speculation and prophecy for fact. Nothing is ever as inevitable as this proposition asserts. Indeed, given the well-dispersed global knowledge of what even a limited nuclear war would entail, it can be argued that such a possibility makes non-nuclear war less likely to escalate. Further, war is not an all-or-nothing condition. Rather, war forms part of a global continuum of violence, extending from isolated acts of terrorism to insurrection to conventional war and then, finally, to nuclear use.

However, this continuum neither disappears nor changes its essential nature by the addition of the Bomb at one end. In fact, quite the opposite occurs. The enormity of the destruction, the futile destruction, inherent in any use of nuclear weaponry actually reifies the non-nuclear portion of the continuum. The ability to wage effective sub-nuclear war assumes a new and unique importance. Given this ability, and its prudent and limited use, escalation actually becomes less likely. Further still, across most of this continuum of violence, the nuclear factor is simply irrelevant. Or, to state it another way: the reasons why nations (and movements) fight have not and will not change one iota. Only the consequences of certain actions, and of certain failures, are affected. No Vietcong, no PLO terrorist, no African guerrilla, no Sandinista, no Cuban "volunteer" ever laid down his arms—or changed his ideology—because of the remote possibility of nuclear war. Nor are very many likely to; the causes and disciplines which impel them remain (in their eyes, at least) both valid and in force. Atomic weaponry cancels no class division, no civil struggle, no boundary dispute, no political, economic, or racial antagonism. Rather, such weaponry adds another dimension to the continuum of conflict which may or may not be relevant, depending upon the circumstances and the skill and prudence of the nuclear powers. Thus, to argue that because such weapons exist, they must inevitably be used within the context of escalating lesser conflicts, is no more logical to suggest than crossing a busy street automatically entails an unacceptable risk of being run over.

To be sure, however, unrestrained nuclear warfare obliterates any possible relationship between ends and means. But this (for the present) obscenely final threat to the planet neither determines all other conflicts nor rightly dominates all prudential calculation. Nor does it even negate, as many have argued, the essential morality of deterrence. As the Protestant theologian Paul Ramsey has well written: "To choose liberty by means that could conceivably threaten the existence of mankind, to choose liberty by means that *might* lead to destruction, is not yet the same as choosing death."[14] This distinction, so often overlooked by those who wish to reduce all human aspirations and values to the mindless, terror-stricken howl for pre-emptive nuclear surrender, is crucial. For, not only does it suggest that obsession with nuclear catastrophe can lead to the destruction of other values: it also tends toward a form of intellectual totalitarianism. In totalitarian systems, the power to perform an act equates to both the intention of so doing, and to the inevitability of that act's performance. In a totalitarian state, the mere ability to resist, or to dissent, or to think independently, equates to a criminal act, justifying pre-emptive persecution. In the world of nuclear monomania, the mere possession of nuclear weapons, and their deterrent use, equates to inevitable holocaust. This is shoddy reasoning, at best.

And anyway, as Ramsey has written, not without a certain understated irony: "Deterrence provides what pacifism always sought: a substitute for the use of force."[15] Nuclear weapons, then, do not, by their mere existence, negate either the continuum of conflict or the *jus ad bellum*, at least the *jus ad bellum* as applied to the non-nuclear portion of the continuum. And while the morality of threatening an ultimately immoral act—mass destruction—may be questioned, not even this negates the non-nuclear applications of the heritage.[16] What it does do is to provide a firm statement on the limits of just war: when unrestricted nuclear exchange begins, *but not before*.

A second argument against the use of the just war vocabulary carries a bit more intellectual weight. According to this position, the *jus ad bellum* already exists, albeit in a severely truncated form, in contemporary international law, and that law (as presently codified) provides adequate guidance for both individuals and states. This reasoning upholds a basic premise of contemporary international law: that nations may resort to arms only in individual or collective self-defense, and then only in response to a prior and clearly defined act of territorial aggression. In effect, this formulation (as found in both the Nuremburg decisions and the United Nations Charter) declares that response to physical invasion constitutes the only legitimate *casus belli*, adding the implicit corollary that if everyone is forbidden to shoot first, no one will shoot at all.

On the surface, this seems an eminently logical piece of reductionism, and quite in keeping with allegedly traditional American values. First shot equals aggression; aggression equates to international crime; defense thus automatically acquires both legitimacy and limitation—the limitation of repelling the aggressor, but no more. All in all, a tidy little formulation in which the only relevant question becomes, "Who started it?"

The problem with this argument is twofold. First, it ignores the existence of a continuum of conflict, especially the exceedingly complex twentieth century continuum. Few modern conflicts ever exhibit such an unambiguous character. "Who started it?" is rarely as simple a question as "Who fired first?" Further, most contemporary conflicts exhibit a "mixed" character: part civil war, part ideological struggle, part international (or proxy) war. In such cases, the question of who fired first may prove not only irrelevant, but also impossible to determine.[17]

Further still, the law ignores the whole issue of the humanitarian use of military force. Writing in *Just and Unjust Wars*, Michael Walzer (an unrepentant former anti-Vietnam activist) condemns what he calls the "legalist paradigm"—the restriction of justifiable violence to self-defense—as both inhumane and unrealistic. Indeed, Walzer finds himself in the odd position of advocating occasional interventions in order to prevent crimes such as genocide:

> Any state capable of stopping the slaughter has a right,

at least, to try to do so. The legalist paradigm indeed rules out such efforts, but that only suggests that the paradigm, unrevised, cannot account for the moral realities of military intevention.[18]

"The moral realities of military intervention"—surely an interesting phrase from the pen of a left-leaning Harvard professor. But Walzer is correct in recognizing, just as had Saint Augustine, that humanitarian intervention on behalf of others can indeed constitute just cause.

But the legalist paradigm does not comprise the whole of international law, and in recent years the law itself has been moving away from such artificial simplicity. Obviously, the legalist paradigm is a formulation intended for a world of well-defined territorial sovereignties: nation-states which, at least in theory, are obliged to respect each other's borders and acknowledge each other's right to regulate their own internal affairs. But the world is not composed entirely of nation-states, and international law now attempts to deal with these various non-sovereign entities. Unfortunately, however, the law has itself become "unjust," establishing, in effect, one standard for sovereignties, and another for so-called revolutionary movements. Since the 1970's, a number of treaties and formulations have attempted to extend the rights of belligerency to "struggles of peoples against colonial, alien, and racist regimes," as in the 1977 "Protocols Additional to the Geneva Convention of 1949"—a treaty signed by President Carter but, as of this writing, mercifully unratified.[19] This movement to legitimize the *competence de guerre* of every terrorist or insurrectionary group that might claim for itself the status of freedom fighter (and who would not?), if carried to its logical extreme, would establish an unconscionable double standard: one set of rules (the legalist paradigm) for sovereignties, and another for so-called liberation movements. How this new formulation might be applied in a world where most such movements, by virtue of their clandestine nature and military weakness, could not afford to obey the *jus in bello*, remains a matter of considerable uncertainty. But if it is indeed true that hypocrisy is the tribute that vice pays to virtue, then the nations of the Marxist and Third Worlds, by advancing this double standard in the United Nations and elsewhere, may have done us all a favor. They have reaffirmed that the notion of just cause matters, and that the legitimate use of force may not be restricted to territorial self-defense, whether individual or collective. And it would be regrettable, were this revival of interest in just war to work for the sole benefit of non-democratic entities, while the democratic states forgot its truth, and endangered their own existence thereby.

CODA: THE WEINBERGER DOCTRINE

On November 28, 1984, Secretary of Defense Caspar Weinberger delivered a speech at the National Press Club, Washington, D.C.[20] The speech was entitled, "The Uses of Military Power," and was intended to suggest a series of criteria to be met prior to any use of American military force. Secretary Weinberger distinguished six criteria:

1) Force should be used only to protect vital interests.

2) Force should not be used unless it is adequate to achieve success.

3) Force should serve clearly defined objectives.

4) The relationship between objectives and the use of force must be readjusted as necessary during conflict, in order to achieve success.

5) There must be reasonable assurance, prior to commitment, that both Congress and the people support this action.

6) Commitment of force should be a last resort.

It is probable that Secretary Weinberger has never studied the *jus ad bellum* in any great detail: its historical development, its arcana, its nuances. But the doctrine he suggested in his National Press Club speech most certainly reflects this heritage: just cause, right intent, competent authority, proportionality of means to ends, the last-resort nature of war. The specific vocabulary may differ; the insight does not.

Indeed, if Secretary Weinberger departed from the heritage in any significant way, it was only to make explicit one point which no previous just war had ever found it necessary to do:

The idea that, once force is committed, it is both necessary and prudent to succeed.

Responses to the Claim:
Resistance, Evasion, Consent

He may decide that his commander, his army, or his people may justly demand his life, but may not command him to do what is in violation of his deepest self.

J. Glenn Gray
The Warriors

In the last chapter, I suggested two things. First, that the *jus ad bellum* provides a basic working vocabulary by which and through which citizen and democratic state may communicate on matters pertaining to war and the bearing of arms. Secretary Weinberger's speech was one such communication, albeit one which used the general categories of the heritage rather than the specific terminologies. To be sure, the *jus ad bellum* provides no convenient catalogue of just causes, no repertoire of right intents, no clear, universally applicable definition of competent authority, no all-purpose indicator of last resort, no unarguable prudential calculus for the nuclear age, and no unassailable guide to proportionality in the terrorist/insurrectionary era. Men and women of good will and high morality can and will disagree on the specifics. But the heritage does reaffirm, as has international law of late, that there exist reasons for fighting beyond individual or communal physical self-preservation: reasons which, in a democratic, pluralistic society, must be defined by individual and state by constant dialogue. In equal measure, the *jus ad bellum* reaffirms that the unlimited, promiscuous use of force, while perhaps understandable *in extremis*, in situations of what Walzer calls "supreme emergency," is rarely justified.[1] Certainly, the unrestricted use of nuclear weapons never can be condoned.

Second, I have suggested that there are individuals and political entities who cannot rightly avail themselves of this vocabulary; their creeds, intents and fanaticisms proscribe it. Some are religious or political crusaders, holding that the employment of force on behalf of their particular causes or obsessions need know no bounds. Others are indiscriminate pacifists, holding that warfare is always and forever unacceptable to them. Juridically, these refusants have been known as conscientious objectors: a legal category which, until about two decades ago, applied only to those who avowed an unequivocal, indiscriminate opposition to all forms of war, based upon their understanding of the will of God. Since then, both legally and culturally, this category has been expanded to include numerous other categories of objection, and it is my purpose in this chapter to argue that even though such objection may well correspond to the imperatives of the *jus ad bellum*, the legal right of conscientious objection—*the right to exemption from the consequences of dissent*—should be abolished. There is irony here, and sadness, and the inevitability of personal tragedy. Yet it must be done, and should be done before the next use of force, if this country is to survive as a moral entity.

To explain:

The traditional, i.e., the indiscriminate conscientious objector, has been the man (or, occasionally, woman) who declines not only to serve, but also to acknowledge any possible moral rightness in service, regardless of the exigencies that may mandate it. Historically, such persons have had a great deal to say in justification of their chosen stance. In the American context, such persons have usually been accorded a great deal of respectful attention. And, more often than not, these Americans have received the exemptions and immunities they sought. Over the past quarter-century, however, a new form of pacifism, and of pacifist, has arisen: an historically unprecedented phenomenon which has managed (not without a bit of help from the mass media) to obscure the fact that military service can be an act at least as moral as refusal. This new pacifism has created an ethical one-sidedness to the issue that can no longer be allowed. In its legal context, this new pacifism has warped the traditional American practice of according immunity to the point where the right must now be extended to virtually everyone, or else abolished entirely.

It is time to realign the continuum of value that decrees refusal somehow intrinsically superior to acceptance, and resistance somehow more virtuous than consent. In order to do so, and in order to justify the need for the abolition of conscientious objector rights, it is necessary to reaffirm a distinction which never should have been lost: the difference between the transcendent conscience and the exercise of mere dissent. It is time, in short, to take a new look at much of what passes for conscience in contemporary America. More importantly, it is time to recover the idea of conscience as a human faculty which includes consent as well as opposition, and which reaffirms consent as, in most cases, the proper and moral response to the military claim.

TRANSCENDENCE OR DISSENT?

"I believe," wrote Michael Harrington during the Vietnam War, "that a democratic society should not require its citizens to violate their deeply held principles."[2] Surely a reasonable statement, this contention that a government of, by, and for the people ought not to degrade its citizens by coercing them in ways they find morally abhorrent. And yet, this statement, so proper on its face, leaves unanswered, and indeed never even asks, three critical questions.

First, what are "deeply held principles?" Is a deeply held principle the same thing as a conscience? And how is depth to be determined?

Second, are all deeply held principles, or even all consciences, entitled to equal consideration? Are all equally valid, at least insofar as they pertain to the bearing of arms?

Third, in a world where human beings live in polities, especially pluralistic polities, in a world where violence remains the ultimate arbiter in the relations of those polities known as states, and in a world of increasing non-state-originated violence, what is the proper balance between individual refusal and national purpose and survival?

A quick trip to the dictionary reveals conscience to be: "The faculty of recognizing the distinction between right and wrong in regard to one's own conduct," and also: "Conformity to one's own sense of conduct."[3] A thoroughly unexceptional definition which, unfortunately, omits one item that has puzzled theologians, philosophers, psychologists, and jurists for millennia: Just where does conscience come from? The definition simply posits its existence, *sui generis* and complete unto itself, no matter what its origin or content, and leaves it at that.

No greater misinterpretation of conscience could exist: a misinterpretation especially pernicious in matters of military service and war.

Throughout history, conscience related to the bearing of arms has taken a variety of forms: personal honor, chivalry, patriotism, ideological and religious justification, legal codes of conduct, the entire just war heritage, and conscientious objection. It is worth noting that, of all these categories (and more could be adduced), all but one pertains to those actually or potentially engaged in military activity. Equally noteworthy is the fact that these categories reflect more than simple personal preference. Even private honor, that "enigmatic blend of conscience and ego," acknowledges values beyond individual preference and choice. Historically, these categories reflect a wide variety of political, social, military, and legal arrangements. They are, in short, based as much upon communal values as upon individual sensibility or whim. They reflect an interplay between the conscience of the individual who bears arms and the laws and mores of the polity he protects.

The warrior's conscience, then, neither stands alone nor exists without specific, often legally defined content.

In equal measure, the conscience of the indiscriminate, theistic (usually Christian) objector recognizes the need of a certain commonality of meaning with the larger community. In the schema of the indiscriminate, theistic objector, an absolute prohibition exists. This prohibition derives from his understanding of the desires of the God of the larger society. The objector obeys this transcendent prohibition, as he understands it, and also attempts to communicate his understanding of God's will to the polity. Indeed, the genuine theistic objector must be counted among the most courageous of humans. The man or woman who says, "Do unto me what you will, God, our common God, forbids my participation and I will not participate"—surely this person acknowledges values beyond personal preference, and with a courage akin to that of the warrior.

Such conscientious objectors, however, are rare. And, over the past two decades, the American conscientious objector, as defined by law, has come to present a vastly different problem. Legally, he stands alone. Legally, he has no firm relationship either to society or to God or to anyone or anything outside himself. He speaks only for, and about, himself. It is indeed an ironic, sad condition that, despite the prevalence of such objectors, despite all the attention and support they garner, and despite the arguments they invoke, *legally and morally, they stand alone.*

It was not always so.

As Michael Walzer has correctly pointed out, individual conscience, in order to have political and ethical meaning, must emanate from something more than the individual. It must be based upon an understanding of God's will, or else upon some other transcendent value, which can be communicated to (if not shared by) the larger society. According to Walzer:

> [T]he very word "conscience" implies a shared moral knowledge, and it is probably fair to argue not only that the individual's understanding of God, or of the higher law, is

always acquired within a group, but also that his obligation
to either is at the same time an obligation to the group and
its members. . . . An individual whose moral experiences
never reached beyond "monologue" would know nothing
at all about responsibility, and could have none.[4]

Conscience, then, means literally (as well as etymologically)
"to know with." And yet, "monologue," not "conscience,"
more closely describes the current legal and cultural status of
objection in America. Despite the incessant invocation of
nearly every creed and philosophy under the sun, modern
conscientious objectors speak primarily for, and about, themselves; they engage in a monologue which (with a few notable
exceptions) never takes into account the values, let alone the
survival, of the polity. In order to demonstrate this, it is necessary to consider, first, a brief legal history of American conscientious objection, and second, a truly astonishing disjuncture
in that history: a disjuncture mandated entirely by the Supreme Court of the United States, in flagrant violation of both
the will of Congress and the clear intent of the authors of the
Constitution.

CONSCIENCE WITHOUT CONTENT

In the Western tradition, the refusal to bear arms is among
the more recent proscriptions of conscience. There is appar-
ently no record of anyone being persecuted for religious pacifism prior to the advent of Christianity.[5] Even the Jews, who
adamantly refused to serve in the Roman army, did so because of unwillingness to violate the Sabbath and not from any
conviction regarding war. Historically, individual refusal to
bear arms has been associated primarily with Christianity or,
more precisely, with a certain interpretation of Christian duty
which, since the latter days of the Roman Empire, has never

commanded majority assent. Nonetheless, those Christians who divided (and still divide) on this issue remained and remain adherents of the same transcendence. At least in a minimal way, the pacifist and non-pacifist segments of Christianity have always been able to "know together." By the eighteenth century, however, indiscriminate pacifism had become the spiritual preserve of a few peripheral sects, such as the Quakers. Never have these groups constituted more than a tiny fraction of any Western polity.

The United States, since the moment of its birth, has made provision for the membership of such sects. On July 18, 1775, the Continental Congress, in its resolution establishing what would become the first American national army, avowed that:

> As there are people who, *from religious principles, cannot bear arms in any case*, this Congress intend no violence to their consciences, but earnestly recommend it to them to contribute liberally in this time of universal calamity, to the relief of their distressed brethren in the several colonies, and to do all other services to their oppressed Country, which they can, consistently with their religious principles . . .[6] (Italics added)

This general policy of according exemption to the membership of what would become known in American law as "well-recognized peace sects" continued into the twentieth century. The World War I formula was simple. Membership in such a group, coupled with evidence of personal adherence to the group's pacifistic tenets, relieved the objector of military (but not alternative) service. In all cases, the individual remained, and was treated as, a citizen of the endangered polity which had, despite the peril, graciously chosen to honor his scruples. This policy of gracious exemption was upheld by the Supreme Court in the 1918 *Selective Draft Law Cases*, and again in 1931. In all cases, the legal reasoning behind the exemption was clear:

The conscientious objector is relieved from the obligation to bear arms in obedience to no constitutional provision, express or implied, but because, and only because, it has accorded with the policy of Congress thus to relieve him.[7]

During the Second World War, a conflict that engaged far more of America's human resources than the First, Congress not only renewed, but also expanded the privilege of exemption by awarding it to anyone who (regardless of peace sect membership) was "by reason of religious training and belief . . . conscientiously opposed to participation in war in any form."[8] In fact, this was no radical departure; during World War I, President Wilson, had, by Executive Order, extended the exemption privilege to non-peace sect objectors. The World War II draft act simply codified the extension. Henceforward, under the law, any American who grounded his refusal to serve in any war upon his personal understanding of Judeo-Christian writ—an understanding shared by only a small fraction of his endangered fellow countrymen—could qualify for exemption. He would still remain part of the larger polity, subject to noncombatant or alternative service (or prison, should he refuse such service). But he would be spared the direct personal necessity of bearing arms against the Axis in a conflict he'd decreed less important than his personal understanding of the will and word of God. Still, it must be said: both the indiscriminate objector and the larger polity had "known together." The content of the objector's conscience was both open and understandable; the larger polity, although not sharing the contents of that conscience, had found sufficient commonality to justify accepting it.

In 1965, this changed. And with this change came a new, historically unprecedented, definition of conscience as it relates to the bearing of arms. In 1965, by order of the United States Supreme Court, conscience ceased to have any definable content, or even communicable coherence, at all. And with this change came a shift (in the legal sense) from "knowing together" to "monologue."

It is often said that hard cases made bad law. Few Supreme Court decisions bear this out more eloquently than *United States v Seeger*. In this case, fraught with potentially disastrous constitutional implications, the Court attempted to determine which "deeply held principles" qualified their holders for exemption, i.e., which principles would henceforward constitute conscience: which principles the state would be obliged to honor in the discharge of its constitutional obligation to provide for the common defense.

The Supreme Court's determination: *Any and all*, provided that the claimant was "sincere."

Specifically, a certain Mr. Seeger (and, in a companion case, a certain Mr. Jakobson) demanded exemption on religious grounds. Neither professed membership in any well-recognized religious denomination, pacifist or otherwise. Nor did they claim belief in God. Mr. Seeger "preferred to leave the question as to his belief in a Supreme Being open," but assured the Selective Service and the Court that " 'his skepticism or disbelief in the existence of God' did 'not necessarily mean lack of faith in anything whatsoever.' " Rather, Mr. Seeger claimed " 'belief in and devotion to goodness and virtue for their own sakes, and a religious faith in a purely ethical creed.' " Mr. Jakobson, for his part, spoke of a " 'Supreme Reality,' " and defined religion as " 'the sum and essence of one's basic attitude toward the fundamental problems of human existence.' " He also added that " 'Godness' " was " 'the Ultimate Cause for the fact of the Being of the Universe.' "[9]

In its decision, the Supreme Court granted conscientious objector status to Seeger and Jakobson. In so doing, the Court laid down a new principle which now constitutes the legal definition of conscience as it applies to the bearing of arms: to the matter of who shall serve and who shall be exempt; who shall suffer in war, and who not; who shall live, and who shall die. According to the Supreme Court:

> The test of religious belief within the meaning of the exemption . . . is whether it is a *sincere* and *meaningful* belief occupying in the life of its possessor a place *parallel to that filled by the God of those admittedly qualified for the exemption.* . . . Local boards and courts are to decide whether the objector's beliefs are *sincerely held* and whether they are, *in his own scheme of things*, religious; they are not to require proof of the religious doctrines *nor are they to reject beliefs because they are not comprehensible.*[10] *(Italics added)*

In seeming deference to the specific wording of the Universal Military Training and Service Act (although not to the Founding Fathers), the Court added that: "The exemption does not cover those who oppose war from a merely personal moral code."[11] The precise difference between "one's own scheme of things" and the "merely personal," the Court did not bother to define.

What the Supreme Court of the United States here decreed was, in effect, that the test of conscience would be "sincerity." Conscience could have no definable content, and need not exhibit any coherent content at all. Henceforward, the conscience of the devout Quaker, or Catholic, or Buddhist, would be equivalent to that of the agnostic professing belief in "Godness," or the atheist professing belief in whatever religion-equivalent he might come up with, or the lunatic acting in response to last night's hallucination, or to a commandment once encountered on a men's room wall. Henceforward, "deeply held principles" would be coterminous with conscience, and conscience would be whatever the holder said it was, provided he said it with sufficient sincerity. And so long as the sincerity was adequately intense, the polity would be bound, in this life-and-death matter, to honor all such claims.

The Supreme Court, however, did not stop at *Seeger*. Five years later, in *Welsh v United States*, the Court both reaffirmed and expanded the exemption. In this case, a certain Mr. Welsh petitioned for conscientious objector status, avowing " 'conscientious scruples against participating in wars where people are killed.' "[12] (Would Mr. Welsh, I wonder, have participated in wars where people *aren't* killed?) Mr. Welsh was held to be sincere. However, his local draft board and lower courts had denied his claim because Mr. Welsh characterized his beliefs as "non-religious,' " and derived from " 'reading in the fields of history and sociology' "—a clear disqualification according to extant draft law, which disallowed claims based upon "political, sociological, or philosophical views or a merely personal moral code."[13] Seemingly, the claim was also invalidated by the strictures laid down in *Seeger*. Indeed, Mr. Welsh explicitly disavowed any religious connotations or congruencies at all. As he told the Court:

> "I believe I mentioned taking of life as not being for me, a religious wrong. . . . My decision arises from what I believe to be considerations of validity from the standpoint of the welfare of humanity and the preservation of the democratic values which we in the United States are struggling to maintain. I have concluded that war, from the practical standpoint, is futile and self-defeating, and that from the more important moral standpoint, it is unethical."[14]

The Supreme Court awarded conscientious objector status to Mr. Welsh, despite his denials, and despite the clear intent of Congress that such persons not be granted the exemption. In so doing, the Court claimed that Mr. Welsh's beliefs *were* "religious," as *they* had intended the word, and noted:

> In view of the broad scope of the word "religious," a registrant's characterization of his beliefs as "non-religious" is not a reliable guide to those administering the exemption.

. . . We think this attempt [to invoke *Seeger* as grounds for denial] . . . fails for the reason that *it places undue emphasis on the registrant's interpretation of his own beliefs.*[15] (Italics added)

"Undue emphasis on the registrant's interpretations of his own beliefs"—in the matter of individual conscience? Thus the law of the land: from "knowing together" to individual "sincerity," whether comprehensible or not, and thence to the Supreme Court's determination that only *they* were qualified to pass judgment on who meant what. There are, no doubt, many millions of consciences in America today. There are also, no doubt, many coherent, communicable, deeply held principles. But, in the legal sense, conscience as it pertains to the bearing of arms has become *de facto* meaningless. The privilege of exemption from military service must now be opened to virtually anybody, or else abolished entirely.

I favor the latter alternative. Since the ratification of the Bill of Rights two centuries ago, conscientious objector immunities have been based upon that portion of the First Amendment which prohibits interference with the free exercise of religion. Clearly, this prohibits forcing any traditional objector to bear arms. But such persons can, in this matter, freely exercise their religion from a prison cell, as well as from some alternative work assignment. In equal measure, non-traditional indiscriminate objectors should also be prepared to accept the consequences of their refusal. It is one thing to refuse; it is quite another to expect and demand exemption from the consequences of one's refusal.

And, in the end, is not individual willingness to accept the consequences of one's actions the true mark of conscience?

THE CONSCIENCE OF CONSENT

It is necessary now to consider the conscience which declares itself willing to bear arms in the common defense.

Throughout human history, people have borne arms for a variety of reasons: exalted, base, pragmatic, self-destructive, inane. Many have served simply because their polities decreed it, submitting to conscription with (in the words of one Vietnam veteran) "a kind of sleepwalking default."[16] Today, however (we are told), conscription need no longer defile the national conscience. The volunteer quotas are being met. The problem has been solved.

The problem has not been solved. Nor will the problem be solved until this nation regains an understanding of the moral aspect of the decision to bear arms, of that act of conscience which alone transforms state claim into individual obligation. For over a decade now, both the memory of Vietnam and the ostensible success of the yet-untested-in-combat All-Volunteer Force (AVF) have tended to obscure the actual nature of this act of conscience. The military shortcomings, real and potential, of the AVF will be considered in the final section of this book. For now, it is necessary to reaffirm that the conscience of consent is not the same thing as patriotism, an emotion which can legitimately be felt (and invoked) by the most ardent pacifist. Nor is the conscience of consent the same as submission to the will of the state. It is something else, and something more.

Since the founding of the American Republic, it has been a commonplace that this polity reflects the thinking of John Locke. The Lockean concept of social contract, of the act of political constitution which binds individuals together, implies a world of common purposes and shared values. In the Lockean schema, individuals constantly re-ratify the social contract in numerous ways. First, they remain members of the commonwealth established by the social contract (in this case, the Constitution). Second, they accept the benefits of living in the commonwealth. Third, they give their tacit consent to the commonwealth's existence by obeying its laws, including those pertaining to military service. As Locke wrote nearly three centuries ago.

> . . . every man, that has any possession, or enjoyment of any part of the dominions of any government, does thereby give his *tacit consent*, and is as far forth obliged to obedience to the laws of that government, during such enjoyment, as any one under it.[17]

Not quite "Love It or Leave It," but, as Harry Jaffa, writing in 1982 on draft registration, applied the theory:

> Those who do not become members of a body politic at its institution, are nonetheless voluntary members by consenting to remain within it. . . . [E]veryone reaching the age of consent, who consents to remain, consents at the same time to obey the laws founded upon that consent. . . . [S]afety is the condition for the enjoyment of all the peaceful fruits of society. The voluntary association called the body politic is nothing unless it is an agreement that no one need defend himself alone, but that henceforth each shall be defended by all. But each cannot be defended by all, unless all are defended by each.[18]

In the Lockean tradition, then, military service flows naturally from residence, from acceptance of benefits, and from obedience to the laws, including those laws which determine who shall serve, for how long, where, when, and why.

This is wrong.

No, not wrong, exactly. Just grievously incomplete. For military service is, in reality, the antithesis of the acceptance of benefits. Certainly, it is so for those who don't choose it voluntarily. Military service is, in fact, an activity quintessentially different and set apart from all other activities. It involves the possibilities of uprooting, hardship, suspension of life plans, suffering, disfigurement, death, and the commission of acts otherwise morally abhorrent and always scarring. The military claim is unique. No other demand that a polity makes—for taxes, for labor, for obedience—can rival it in either severity of hardship or possible consequences. It may indeed be correct to argue, for example, that use of the public highways obliges one to obey the rules of the road, but it is preposterous to suggest that a few years spent on the interstate system (or accepting other benefits) can obligate one to suffer, kill, and die. If the military claim is to have any moral validity for the individual, it must be based upon more than acceptance of benefits, or mere residence, or mere obedience. It must be based upon a clear recognition of the unique nature of the claim—especially the contemporary American claim—and of the special individual consent which alone can turn claim into obligation.

A democratic state, as already argued, may legitimately decree that some or all of its members bear arms. A democratic state may justly punish those who refuse. By making the military claim, this democratic state is simply fulfilling the mandate of the Constitution to provide for the common defense. But the obligation to bear arms comes into existence only when the individual consents: a consent required even in the induction ceremony, which requires the draftee to take one step forward before the oath may be administered. Indeed, the oath itself specifies that the obligation is undertaken freely; the inductee swears that he does in fact consent to serve. What that oath, and that step forward, signify, or ought to signify, is far more than "sleepwalking default." Both acts should signify the resolution of a profound and universal moral dilemma, a problem best codified by the Protestant theologian Paul Ramsey:

> The individual is included within the common good of the
> nation-state . . . but he is *not* included in the national com-
> mon good *to the whole extent of his personhood.* The per-
> son transcends the political community, but again, not to
> the whole extent of his being.[19] (Italics Ramsey's)

The conscience of consent involves the striking of a balance
between the legitimate demand of the democratic state and
the personal and ethical reticence of the citizen upon whom
the demand is made. The conscientious consentor knows, as
does the objector, that his own sense of right and wrong must
remain his final *arbiter, as that sense of right and wrong pertains to his own conduct.* Unlike the objector, however, he also
recognizes the existence of a polity in need of, and worthy of,
his participation in its physical defense. He admits the significance of the polity into his judgment of his own proper conduct. He does not transfer his conscience to the state, nor
does he claim that the state may license him to do anything on
its behalf. Rather, he shares his conscience with the polity. He
permits its laws and purposes to inform his own. When the
conscientious consentor agrees to bear arms, he transcends
himself for the purpose of the common defense: transcends
himself, in part. He establishes a balance that endures until
the polity either no longer requires his services, or else breaks
faith with him so flagrantly that service become impossible.

The conscientious individual who consents to serve knows
full well that this breach of faith may well come to pass. He
knows, as Robert Tucker has written:

> The only certainty once force is employed is the destruc-
> tion of values. Against this certainty can be placed only the
> possibility—it is never more than a possibility—that the
> values to be preserved will justify the suffering and destruc-
> tion caused by war.[20]

In sum, the conscientious individual who consents to serve

says more than, *I will.* He also says, *Credo.* I believe. I believe that this polity, of which I am a part, deserves my participation in its physical defense.

SELECTIVE DISSENT

But what if the conscientious consentor finds himself unable to consent? What if the conscientious individual, especially the individual who employs the logic and the vocabulary of the *jus ad bellum*, finds himself unable to serve in particular places or capacities? What if he decides that, although he feels no objection to military service in the abstract, the specific service required of him cannot in good conscience be performed? Might he not be entitled to exemption on the basis of his understanding of the *jus ad bellum*, just as indiscriminate objectors are entitled to exemption on the basis of whatever notions strike them as valid?

In 1971, the Supreme Court decreed that he is not. In *Gillette v United States*, the Court held that, although indiscriminate objectors could be afforded exemption for literally any reason on earth (given sufficient sincerity), citizens who employed the just war heritage as a guide to their own decisions had no such right.

In other words, although the just war heritage provides the only commonality of meaning available to us, its use as grounds for refusal is utterly illegal.

And so it should be: tragically, ironically illegal. As the Court correctly noted, no nation which permits its citizens to pick and choose their wars *without penalty* can expect to survive.[21] This must be as true for selective as for indiscriminate objectors. In both cases, willingness to accept the consequences of one's refusal must be deemed the true and final test of conscience. Otherwise, conscience becomes a mere refuge for the lazy, the cowardly, the narrowly self-interested, and the opportunistic. It is indeed deplorable that men of good will and high principle should suffer, in order that conscientious objection not be used in this manner. But it is also necessary, and if the prevention of such use is made possible by the prison terms of the genuine, then the genuine objectors, indiscriminate and selective, may indeed make thereby a contribution to the survival of the polity they have chosen not to defend, in some circumstances, or in all.

CODA: THE PROBLEM OF HOBBES

On January 5, 1985, an Op-Ed column headlined, "I Won't Register for the Draft," appeared in the *New York Times.* The column, written by a Mr. Andy Mager, announced the following:

That he was about to go on trial for refusal to register for the draft.

That he had voluntarily informed the Selective Service System of his refusal, thereby inviting prosecution.

That he had chosen to represent himself, and not use the defense of selective prosecution (deemed as constitutional by the Supreme Court), in order that the issues involved might be made as clear as possible.

According to Mr. Mager.

> Draft registration can be an initial step in the national process of preparing for war. My beliefs lead me to feel that I should not participate in preparations for war in any way. . . . I believe war is an immoral way to attempt to settle conflict, and today conventional war, which can quickly escalate into nuclear war, may well be suicidal. If President Reagan decides to send troops to Nicaragua, I will not be among them. . . . Complicated legal arguments would only obscure my primary argument: that war must end . . .[22]

Mr. Mager also noted that he had been sustained in his decision both by those known to him personally, and by examples of similar refusals in other countries. He concluded with a paragraph indicating that he felt he acted within a venerable American tradition.

Now, it is undeniable that there is something both admirable and awe-inspiring about a person who, in the service of his beliefs, accepts—indeed, invites—the consequences. Assuming that the information contained in Mr. Mager's column is correct (which I have no reason to doubt), he is clearly an exceptional young man. By seeking prosecution, he has demonstrated his commitment beyond all question. By rejecting both legal counsel and technical defenses, he has made the issue explicit. And although he does not reveal the sources of his belief, it is apparent that his is a conscience in the sense of "knowing together." He wishes to speak to others, not evade them, and, far from seeking exemption from the consequences of his refusal, he positively demands imprisonment. He seems to be an altogether admirable person.

But for a polity to survive, it is not enough that its citizens be conscientious, or admirable, or even right—as Mr. Mager surely is when he states that "war must end." Nor is it simply enough to refuse to serve, and then to decree it a service to the polity, in the hope that it will somehow advance those abstractions known as universal peace and justice. On the surface, Mr. Mager's argument seems as admirable as his courage. Looked at a bit more deeply, however, two problems arise: problems which, when extended to the polity as a whole, prove so dangerous that the polity may rightly punish the former, and take other measures to correct the latter.

The first of these problems might be called the practice of pre-emptive dissent. Mr. Mager objects to what "might" happen. Registration "might" be a preparation for war. Troops "might" go to Nicaragua (or elsewhere). Armageddon "might" result. The issue of substituting one's self-proclaimed gift of prophecy for fact has already been discussed. It is unacceptable as an all-purpose excuse for refusal to serve. And it is exceedingly common these days; indeed, it has been something of a cultural fad since Vietnam. This pre-emptive selective objection appears every time a young man refuses to register on the grounds of what "might" happen: Armageddon, another Vietnam, future intervention somewhere or other. Every young man who declares himself "ready to fight" should the Russians invade, but then refuses to train for such an eventuality on the premise that his services "might" be abused elsewhere, avails himself of this evasion.

It is intolerable. Whatever the tenets of the just war heritage, it does not authorize individuals to substitute speculation for conscience, or for fact. And while an individual already in uniform may, as a matter of conscience, determine that he cannot serve in some particular capacity (and justifiably endure the consequences), he may not do so pre-emptively and abstractly.

But were all such pre-emptive dissent based upon Mr. Mager's reasoning, the danger to the polity would not be all that severe. Individuals such as Mr. Mager are rare, and a necessary component of public dialogue. But this form of pre-emptive refusal has, in recent years, been coupled to what can only be described as trendy neo-Hobbesianism: a phenomenon which represents, not conscience or courage, but simple animal fear elevated to the status of an ethical absolute.

In the philosophy of Thomas Hobbes (one of Locke's contemporaries), the primary human emotion and motivation is stark terror, and the pre-emptive anxieties attendant thereon. Existence is the ultimate value: not the precondition for other values, but an absolute end in itself. "For every man," wrote Hobbes three centuries ago, "is desirous chiefly of what is good for him and shuns what is evil, but chiefly the chiefest of natural evils, which is death."[23] In order to avoid physical extinction and perpetual terror, those ineluctable byproducts of the state of nature's "war of all against all," men form societies. They form them, according to Hobbes, for the purpose of individual self-preservation, and for no other primary reason:

> The final cause, end, or design of men (who naturally love liberty and dominion over others), is the introduction of that restraint upon themselves (in which we see them live in commonwealths) in the foresight of their own preservation . . .[24]

Since the sole legitimate purpose of government is the perpetuation of each individual's survival, any state which threatens, or seems to threaten (in Hobbes' schema, the two equate) such survival, forfeits the obedience and loyalty of its citizens. No state, according to Hobbes, may legitimately demand that a single individual die, or risk his life, or even endure fear, since that would be to negate the state's sole *raison d'être*. And every individual, when confronted by such a demand, may rightfully resist, evade, or ignore it, or unilaterally seek such terms as he can get from real, potential, or imagined enemies.

To be sure, Hobbes recognized that a society so founded would be based upon a gigantic fraud, protecting its members only so long as no danger threatened, its bonds and power disintegrating in sight of peril. Indeed, Hobbes so feared this outcome that he concluded:

> . . . when the defense of the Commonwealth requires at once the help of all that are able to bear arms, everyone is obliged; because otherwise the institution of the Commonwealth, which they have not the purpose, or the courage, to protect, was in vain.[25]

Yet, among those categories of citizen whom Hobbes exempted from military service were those afflicted with "natural timorousnes"—in effect, the conscientiously cowardly.[26]

In the Hobbesian sense, fear always remains the final political and moral arbiter, and the fearful, solitary individual the only absolute. Today, three centuries later, this "conscientious cowardice" enjoys a certain vogue. It exists most visibly in the nuclear freeze and unilateral disarmament movements, and in the occasionally resurrected slogan, "Better Red than Dead." Today, it is quite respectable, indeed somewhat trendy, to proclaim one's terror from political rostra, from church pulpits, at cocktail parties, in the media, and on the streets. It is no unusual event for a psychiatrist to assert, as one did on a certain late-night talk show, that the rising suicide rate among high school and college students can be attributed to the fear of nuclear war. Today, in short, it is fashionable to take the ultimate disaster, nuclear war, and convert it into the all-purpose excuse.

And thus the first of the two problems raised by Mr. Mager's argument: pre-emptive refusal. Mr. Mager himself seems to be no coward. But the tactic of pre-emptive dissent, as practiced today by many of those who seemingly share Mr. Mager's principles, too often draws upon, and indeed flaunts, the Hobbesian "right" of cowardice.

But it is the second problem raised by Mr. Mager's stance which may prove the more troublesome. His argument lacks a certain quality: a quality for which, I would suggest, the English language currently lacks even a proper definition. That quality is not patriotism; if anything, Mr. Mager's argument shows a love of country beyond the norm. Nor is this quality conscience. Rather, it is a quality known to the philosophers of antiquity, and to the America Founding Fathers, as civic, or public, virtue. It is a quality which once found its highest expression in the free man's consent to bear arms.

It is necessary now to explore the nature of this quality of civic virtue, as it was known to the Founding Fathers, and to determine whether it lost all relevance sometime during the Vietnam War.

Part Two

HISTORY

The American Revolution Just Cause, Self-Interest, and the Failure of Ideals

The Revolution is the one component of our past that we have not, at some point or other, explicitly repudiated.

Michael Kammen
A Season of Youth

In the last section, I sketched a basic philosophical framework for the understanding of military service, using the just war tradition (particularly the *jus ad bellum*) as organizing paradigm, and consent as the process by which the individual transforms legitimate state claim into personally binding obligation. I argued that certain types of persons—crusaders given to unlimited violence, indiscriminate pacifists, pre-emptive objectors, and neo-Hobbesians—cannot rightly use this paradigm. I concluded by posing a question: What is the specific human quality that receives its expression in the decision to bear arms? Not simply patriotism, not fanaticism, and certainly not default or mere obedience. But what?

In this section, I shall suggest that this quality has a name, albeit not one normally heard in modern political discourse. In order to demonstrate why this quality, a very old one, has been lost, I shall examine first its place in American history, and then determine the circumstances of its seeming contemporary irrelevance. I shall, again, assert the obvious: that the process of consent does not, cannot, occur in a vacuum. It occurs within the triple contexts of time: of present situations, of possible futures (predicted or merely plausible), and of interpreted (and misinterpreted) pasts. The conscientious consentor, no less than the objector, must reckon with all three. For, when he consents, he does so not only in response to present conditions and exigencies, and to future needs, but also as a legatee of prior refusals and consents, and of their meanings now.

He does so, in short, as a legatee of that still impassioned memory: Vietnam.

But the conscientious individual whose assessment of the past goes no further than Vietnam denies himself an essential amplification, and an essential counterpoint. Vietnam matters, of course, as tragedy, as failure, and as national wound now just beginning to heal. But Vietnam's "lessons" have been so distorted (by all sides) that, taken alone, Vietnam provides neither adequate precedent nor reliable guide. The Vietnam tragedy was, and remains, less a failure of morality than of mind: the product of a truly astonishing inability to understand the significance of what America was trying to do, and why that effort failed. This is *not* to say that America should have intervened in Vietnam; personally, I do not believe that we should have. But it is to say that, unless Vietnam is recognized as an exercise in *mindlessness* unparalleled in American history, it will remain an incomplete and pernicious guide to decision-making at both the individual and policy levels.

Perhaps the only way to escape this mindlessness is to place both its sources and its results within historical context.

But if Vietnam cannot be considered alone, what context might be appropriate? All of America's wars teach their lessons, but only one has resembled Vietnam in its complexities and ambiguities. Which one? Not the World Wars and not (at least until late 1951) Korea. Those struggles, clear-cut responses to well-defined prior aggressions, took place under conditions not likely to recur: ample time to mobilize, supportive public opinion, an inviolable homeland, no nuclear threat. The Civil War? Too peculiarly American in its issues to bear much relevance to the present study. The "expansionist" wars? Again, no: Territorial aggrandizement, like chattel slavery or secession, long ago ceased to be a significant American issue. This leaves only the Revolutionary War, surely an odd pairing for Vietnam. In point of fact, however, it is the American Revolution—its background, precepts, and conduct—which, when counterpointed with Vietnam, proves far more illuminating than comparative study of other wars, at least insofar as questions of military claim and obligation are concerned.

There are two major reasons for this juxtaposition. First, the colonial and Revolutionary periods established what might be termed "the original understanding" on the subject of military service, an understanding which has proven remarkably constant ever since. Second, the Revolutionary ideology, the Founding Fathers' sense of political reality, holds a special relevance for the Vietnam and post-Vietnam eras. For the Founding Fathers well understood that the most deadly threats to freedom can also be the most ambiguous. They also knew that successful resistance to these threats, and indeed the survival of any republic, requires more than patriotism. Freedom and common survival require that the citizenry possess and exercise a quality known to the ancients as civic virtue: a quality much on the minds of the Founding Fathers as they fought their war and established their republic.

It is this quality of civic virtue, as known to the ancients and the Founding Fathers, which constitutes the missing element in the conscience and patriotism and courage of Mr. Mager, *et al.* For, from Aristotle to Machiavelli to Harrington to the framers of the American Constitution, the bearing of arms has been the highest expression of such virtue. Seen as civic virtue, the bearing of arms indicates not submission to the state, not mere self-sacrifice, but the willingness to value the common life, the republic, so highly as to hazard one's own existence on behalf of it and its values.

This civic virtue existed in America until it was squandered —mindlessly, mendaciously, unforgivably squandered—in Vietnam. But it did not exist, and indeed can never exist, on a *purely* voluntary level. Why this is so we shall now consider.

THE HERITAGE

The United States was born in a war. It achieved its independence by force of arms, and the man subsequently revered as the father of his country commanded its first national army. The Revolution, the Founding Fathers, and their cause still elicit, if not the uncritical adulation of the nineteenth century, then certainly enduring admiration and high regard. They've all been enshrined.

Which is to say: They've been denatured, sterilized, and rendered irrelevant thereby.

Michael Kammen may well be right when he suggests that the Revolution, alone among national experiences, has remained (at least in the popular mind) inviolate. But if he is correct, the uncomfortable reason why may be that the period seems to us less compelling than cute: less a living precedent than a costume piece. Indeed, perhaps the most curious aspect of the 1976 Bicentennial was the facile ease with which the invocations and re-enactments took place: brave words, pretty uniforms, but no sense of the moral ambiguities and complexities which the Revolutionary generation had to surmount in order to take up arms against the British Crown.

But if it is true that the fundamental principles of the Founding Fathers still apply, then failure to understand their anguish and limits, as well as their accomplishments, can only result in an impoverished heritage, and in the consequent diminution of American political life. Certainly, this impoverishment manifested itself in much of the opposition to Vietnam. For, despite the obvious differences, both wars had their origins in the question of how to respond to an ambiguous but potentially deadly tyranny. And ironically, in both conflicts, Americans fought, by and large, unwillingly, displaying a reticence found in no other American war. The moral meaning of this reticence was something the Founding Fathers well understood: a moral meaning which post-Vietnam America has yet to address, let alone comprehend.

To explain:

For centuries prior to the colonization of the New World, Englishmen had been accustomed to the concept of the *enforceable* military claim. The archaic Anglo-Saxon *fyrd* (the pre-Norman proto-militia) required the services of every free-man for military training and home defense: a principle subsequently codified in Henry II's *Assize of Arms* (1181), Edward I's *Statute of Winchester* (1285), and Elizabeth I's *Instructions for General Muster* (1572). By the latter sixteenth century, a formal militia structure had emerged, with royally-appointed lord-lieutenants responsible for the organization and training of local units. Every freeman (at least, every freeman who could meet the property qualifications) owed military service as part of his allegiance to the Crown: a debt discharged by periodic training and (presumably defensive) service in war. The freeman was to provide his own weapons and train locally; rank structure within the units would correspond to local social realities. But the obligation would be national, and the purpose was clear: defense of the realm as a whole.

Thus was established, over a period of centuries, the English militia tradition and ideal: the notion that periodic service under arms formed a normal, indeed a virtuous, part of the citizen's life. The militia provided, according to this usage, primarily home defense. In the event of emergencies beyond the militia's capacity to handle, or for extended campaigning outside the country, a *temporary* regular army might be raised: the standard, hideously expensive, always volatile combination of aristocratic officers and scum-of-the-earth soldiery. However, the occasional raising of such forces for specific campaigns would not relieve the citizen of his duty to bear arms.

Ironically, by the seventeenth century, the value of militia against professional formations was beginning to diminish rapidly. But at the very moment when the military utility of part-time citizen-soldiers was becoming, at the very least, questionable, the militia as a political institution acquired a new set of moral meanings. And it was this new set of meanings, as much as the older traditions, which formed the basis of the American pre-Revolutionary understanding of claim and obligation.

Few issues so engaged the seventeenth and eighteenth century English political mind as national defense. The basic question was deceptively simple: Should the protection of the realm be entrusted to a part-time militia, or to a long-service, professional standing army under royal control? At one level, the answer was clear. Professional armies, especially those of the Continental model, were inherently far more effective. But despite (or, perhaps, because of) this superior efficiency, English opinion turned violently against the professional standing army. As Lois Schwoerer has concluded, by the late seventeenth century, there existed a remarkable degree of accord on the subject: "Men of all political persuasions came to believe that a professional, permanent army in the hands of the central government was undesirable."[1] The reason for this profound aversion was not uncritical faith in the fighting abilities of the part-time militia. Nor was it (despite the Cromwellian interlude) simple fear of military dictatorship, a concern aptly described by J. G. A. Pocock as "the small change of the standing army debate."[2] Rather, in the seventeenth and eighteenth centuries, dependence upon—indeed, mere toleration of—a standing professional army was seen as both cause and symptom of a profound decline in the civic virtue of the citizenry. It was this sense of an ineluctable moral nexus between citizenship and military service which formed the basis of the indictment of purely professional, i.e., *voluntary*, forces.

According to this canon (variously called the radical Whig, the radical republican, or the Florentine school of thought), in a "mixed," i.e., a non-despotic state, the citizenry provided a vital counterpoise to the monarchy and the high aristocracy, serving to assure that no group exceeded its constitutional limits. In this theory, the citizenry functioned neither as a source nor an executor of political power, but as a final check upon it. King and Court did not derive their right to rule from the people; they did, however, find their powers and prerogatives lim-

ited by the people's inherent liberties. Any king who invaded
the sphere of those liberties became a tyrant, to be checked or
opposed by the aristocracy or, failing that, by the people at
large. This balance, this ultimate insurance against tyranny,
could only function when the citizenry possessed the quality of
civic (or public) virtue, i.e., the ability and willingness to participate in political life.

The ultimate test of this civic virtue was the ability and willingness to bear arms in defense of liberty. In practice, this
meant two things. First, the citizen had to possess economic
independence, so that his livelihood would never be at the
mercy of another. By definition, this meant ownership of land;
no man dependent upon a salary could ever attain the necessary independence. Second, the citizen had to possess, and be
skilled in the use of, his own weapons. Taken together, these
two factors—land and arms—provided the citizen with the
autonomy necessary for defense of liberty against both foreign
and domestic dangers. Without such autonomy, no real civic
virtue could exist. And without such virtue, no nation could
escape calamity.

Or, as James Harrington put it in *Oceana* three centuries or
so ago: "Men accustomed unto their arms and their liberties
will never endure the yoke."[3]

In this sense, then, the English militia provided far more
than a body of inadequately trained and conditioned part-time
warriors. It also served, at least in theory, as school and guarantor of civic virtue, and as proof of that virtue's existence.
Indeed, to the radical Whig mind, there existed no greater
proof of popular corruption than a citizenry unwilling to bear
arms. Thus, the real evil of a standing army lay not just in its
cost, or in its inherently oppressive potential. The real evil was
that a professional force might induce the citizenry to abandon
its military responsibilities, and thereby lose its civic soul.

In point of fact, however, this theory never quite corresponded to the English reality, and the militia versus standing army debate ended in a compromise which acknowledged the ideal while providing for changing conditions. In 1698, William III gained the right to keep a small peacetime standing army, subject to Parliamentary control. Even though this arrangement effectively removed the issue from practical English politics, radical Whigs such as John Toland and John Trenchard continued a vigorous campaign on behalf of the militia as "school of civic virtue."[4] And it was this mix of theory, pragmatism, and Parliamentary compromise which the American colonists brought with them to the New World and which, until 1775, more or less suited their needs.

At first, colonial militias on the English model made exquisite practical sense. Especially in the early years of any colony's existence, every able-bodied man was required to defend against hostile Indians, and also against Europeans of other nationalities and nefarious intents. Prior to the Revolution, every colony (save Quaker Pennsylvania) established a militia, and their laws display a uniform adherence to the principle of compulsory and—at least in the beginning—universal service.

For two reasons, however, the system never quite worked. First, as any colony grew more settled, military compulsion and military service in general, tended to diminish. Numerous categories of exemption, plus various commutation and substitution arrangements, crept into the laws. Property qualifications for service (never very onerous) were established. Muster days diminished, Enforcement waned. And, as John Shy and Russell Weigley have pointed out, geographical patterns of settlement turned theoretically similar militias into vastly different organizations. In Massachusetts, for example, township-type colonization made it far easier to assemble the militia than in, say, Virginia, with its widely scattered plantations (and slaves to keep an eye on).[5] Of course, also, as danger moved westward during the pre-Revolutionary period, the rationale for readiness moved with it. Except during periods of domestic emergency (and not always then), it became nearly impossible to summon the militia from their homes and occupations. To put it simply: The militiamen, prosperous and comfortable at home, only answered the call when they felt like it. On occasion, the militia couldn't even be summoned to suppress some civil disturbance, since most of the militia were among the rioters.

Thus, over the decades, the universal and compulsory militia system devolved into more of a haphazard training command (and fraternal association) than a serious, responsive, deployable force. And thus arose the second reason for the degradation of the system: When troops were required, it was easier to bypas the militia than to summon it as a unit. Colonial governors in need of troops for distant and extended campaigning might request quotas of volunteers from local units, but such requests often went unfulfilled or ignored. More often than not, colonial governors found themselves in the awkward position of either having to offer enlistment bounties, or to impress the local ne'er-do-well's, or both, Nor did these transient "volunteer militias," recruited *ad hoc* for specific campaigns, usually perform with distinction (a fact not lost upon the British regulars sent to fight in the French and Indian Wars).

In sum, by 1763, the colonial militias (except where a serious Indian threat still existed) had proven themselves almost totally incapable of sustained campaigning, serious training, or even getting the membership out of bed. To be sure, notions of civic virtue still held sway, and in 1773 one Bostonian orator could lament, in good Whig fashion: "It is highly absurd, though not uncommon, that those who have the most to lose by the destruction of a state, should be the least capable of bearing a part in its defense."[6]

The struggle with Great Britain changed all that—in part. The several colonies did indeed field their militias: intermittently, half-heartedly, and, by and large, ineffectively. But the Continental Congress also created the first national army or, to be more precise, created it several times over, since the states (jealous of their own forces and prerogatives) refused to authorize conscription, long-term enlistments, or even adequate bounties and bonuses. True, the United States won its war. But the success was due far more to French assistance and British exhaustion than to American exertions, or even military competence. For the American people displayed a marked reluctance to serve, except for very short periods, usually close to home, and often on rather extortionate financial terms. Between 1775 and 1783, somewhere between 150,000 and 200,000 men saw service, about ten percent of the available white male population.[7] But even this minority took up arms in a manner which (with some exceptions) indicated a far from fervent patriotism, and a panoply of other, not always lofty motives.

When the prospect of armed conflict with Great Britian first became real, the standard colonial response was a fevered attempt to resuscitate the militias. Yet the colonial militias quickly became, and would remain, less an effective fighting instrument than a means of determining and controlling the political attitudes and activities of local populations. Those committed to the revolutionary cause (a small minority) tended to join and remain active; the loyalists tended to flee; and the apathetic majority in the middle usually behaved with whatever passed for expediency at the moment. As John Shy has written:

> When we look more closely at the rebel militia, an interesting if obvious fact confronts us; the prudent, politically apathetic majority of white American males was not eager to serve in the militia, but many of them did nonetheless. . . . Under the circumstances, enrollment in the militia could be a test of loyalty to one side or the other, and it

could be a kind of insurance—the readiest form of insurance in a precarious world.[8]

Thus, the major effect of the militia activations in 1774 and 1775 was not their military improvement, but their politicization and radicalization. And that is how they functioned best during the war: as local guerrilla bands, tying down British regulars, as political police, and as terrorists. Occasionally, these units would win a victory or two against British formations in the open field. For the most part, however, they operated intermittently at home, and not always against the uniformed enemy.

But if the United States was to gain its independence, it had to do more than rely on part-time roving bands. It had to field a national force. In the summer of 1775, the Continental Congress began forming an army under its own direction and control, a rather dubious undertaking for a legislature possessing neither the right to tax nor the power to conscript. The units of the Continental Army were to be drawn from the state militias by Congressionally-assigned (and unenforceable) quotas. Theoretically, a draft of sorts would operate at the state level. In point of fact, the states demurred. Faced with the perennial problem of motivating men to sign on for distant and extended campaigning, the states fell back upon the old expedients. Further, most states proved (not surprisingly) unwilling to offer potential enlistees better terms for Continental than for militia service. Why undercut their own forces in order to support a dubious national army? The result was predictably disastrous for the Continental force, and General Washington's wartime correspondence offers eloquent and exasperated commentary on the subject. A few examples, chosen almost at random:

September 1776, writing to Congress:

The Militia, instead of calling forth their utmost efforts to a brave and manly opposition, in order to repair our Losses, are dismayed, Intractable, and Impatient to return. Great numbers of them have gone off, in some instances almost by whole Regiments . . .

Again to Congress, in September 1776:

The Thirteen Militia Regiments from Connecticut, being reduced to a little more than Seven Hundred Men Rank and file, fit for duty, I have thought proper to discharge the whole, to save the States the immense charge that would arise for officers pay.

To New Jersey Governor William Livingston in 1777:

Sir:
The irregular and disjointed state of the Militia of this Province, makes it necessary for me to inform you, that, unless a law is immediately passed by your Legislature, to reduce them to some order, and to oblige them to turn out, in a different Manner from what they have hitherto done, we shall bring very few into the Field, and even those few will render little or no Service.[9]

For General Washington, only a genuinely national army, its manpower recruited for long terms and by whatever means might prove necessary (including direct conscription) could attain victory. Writing to Congress in September 1776, he concluded:

To place any dependence on Militia is, assuredly, resting on a broken staff. Men just dragged from the tender Scenes of domestick Life; unaccustomed to the din of Arms . . . when opposed to Troops regularly train'd . . . makes them timid, and ready to fly from their own shadows.

The Jealousies of a standing Army, and the Evils to be apprehended from one, are remote; and in my judgment, situated and circumstanced as we are, not to be dreaded . . .[10]

The Congressional response to General Washington's importunings was, however, uniformly negative. Never during the war did Congress authorize multi-year enlistments, which meant that Washington had to raise and discharge armies annually. Nor did Congress ever attempt to offer enlistment terms competitive with state bonuses and bounties. Congress could only request appropriations from the states, and the states were, of course, loath to see their own enlistment incentives overbid at their own expense. Since most states permitted men designated for Continental service to hire substitutes and/or pay commutation fees, avoidance of such service was a relatively simple affair. For those so inclined, enlisting (as opposed to fighting) in the Continental Army became a rather lucrative enterprise. As a latter-day cliche might have phrased it, "Join Early and Often."

Throughout the war, the manpower situation continued to remain, at best, unsatisfactory. Frustrated and dismayed by the ease with which Continental service could be avoided, totally disgusted with the quality of such recruits as came his way, General Washington began to advocate direct conscription from the state militias. Writing to Congress in 1778, he concluded:

> If experience has demonstrated that little more can be done by voluntary inlistments, some other mode must be concerted, and no other presents itself, than that of filling the Regiments by drafts . . .[11]

As late as May 1780, Washington could complain to Patrick Henry that:

> What remains for us to do? Nothing less than furnishing our full quota of Continental Troops, by any means, that will ensure Success.[12]

In October of that year, Washington referred to an "opinion

which seems to have influenced Congress, that men cannot be drafted for the war," and damned it as a "mistaken one"—an expression of frustration quickly followed by the military officer's obligatory apology for having contravened the Congress in its collective wisdom.[13]

Washington, of course, never got national conscription. Nor did he ever get anything resembling the army he needed, and could have created. He fought the war in the classic manner of the weak, husbanding pathetically small forces, winning little victories while avoiding large defeats, waiting the enemy out. And with the peace, and the disbanding of an army that had never quite existed anyway, the utter failure of civic virtue as a mass motivator—indeed the utter failure of the whole notion of an armed citizenry—ceased to matter on the battlefield.

But it did not cease to matter in the deliberations of the Revolutionary veterans soon charged with constituting the polity anew.

THE UNDERSTANDING

It is both ironic and undeniable that the Revolutionary War demonstrated, first to last, the utter inadequacy of the Whig and colonial ideals of citizen service and civic virtue as a source of spontaneous mass motivation. Not only did the state militias prove themselves incapable of sustained (or even intermittent) success against British regulars in the open field; they also failed as a source of usable manpower for the Continental Army. Throughout the war, men fought more for gain (such as it was) than for ideals. Men signed on again and again, accepting substantial bounties for short-term enlistments, which they may or may not have completed before restarting the cycle. The image of the stalwart, long-suffering Continental regular, alas, has its origins more in myth than in reality. In the Revolutionary War, soldiering tended to become a racket, a fact candidly acknowledged by General Washington when he argued in vain for bonuses tied to long-term service, or for direct conscription. But so fragile was the alliance of thirteen sovereign states, so great their mutual jealousies and suspicions, and so acute the political dangers of a protracted war, that Congress never dared take the necessary manpower measures—measures which, ironically, might well have shortened the war by years.

Nor did civic virtue make any sustained appearance among the citizenry at large. There were, to be sure, genuine heroes: perhaps a surprising number in a Confederation of three million people. And, to be sure, revolutions are always made by minorities. But if the military shortcomings of the war serve as any indicator, support for the patriot cause was everywhere less than universal (even after the Loyalist exodus), and usually somewhat less than profound. For this there are, of course, the usual reasons. Given the agrarian society of the eighteenth-century, few men could afford to leave their farms for more than a season. Even the most ardent usually had families to feed, and crops to till, and businesses to run. Nor could the country tolerate it. Further, especially during a long war, the apathetic find it convenient to maintain a certain flexibility; support for the patriot cause varied in proportion to its fortunes and perceived chance of ultimate success—which, for most of the war, weren't good.

More important than necessity and expediency, however, was the nature of the war. For the American Revolution was primarily an *ideological* conflict, the kind of struggle that rarely engages people of purely private concerns, i.e., the great majority. But the Founding Fathers, despite their oft-proclaimed reticence about leaving their homes (the Cincinnatus Syndrome) were far from private men. Rather, they were intensely imbued with the potentialities, and pleasures, and dangers of public life in the Aristotelian sense—the notion that genuine freedom begins when a man leaves the private realm in order to transact the public business among his peers. It has often been argued that the motivations of the Founding Fathers were primarily economic, and indeed there was no segment of the white population which, in one form or another, could not have benefitted economically from independence. Repudiation of planter debts, freedom of trade and industrial production, unimpeded westward migration, all would have had salutary effects. But to argue that men would risk their lives in battle, fight an eight year war, or face the hangman in event of failure, all for purely economic reasons, is absurd—an absurdity which perhaps says more about the economic determinists than about the Founding Fathers. For the Founding Fathers had more on their minds than material gain. They had a strong awareness of the nature of public life, an awareness which (at least as much as economics) drove them to rebellion. For the Founding Fathers held a specific view of human nature, of human motivation, and of the proper ordering of human affairs: a philosophy, by and large, alien to the apathetic of any generation. And it was this philosophy which drove the Founding Fathers to firm conviction of the utter necessity of civic virtue in republican states, even while hard experience convinced them of that virtue's rareness.

To modern ears, the rhetoric of the American Revolution rings slightly hollow; it seems not only quaint, but also excessive. Compared to subsequent upheavals, especially those of the twentieth century, the causes of the American revolt appear almost trivial: a twelve-year litany of colonial over-reaction, hyperbole, pettiness, and bombast. After all, at the beginning of the crisis in 1763, the colonies had just been freed (courtesy of British arms and the British taxpayer) of the French threat. The mother country was deeply in debt, and colonial taxation seemed a reasonable means of defraying the costs of a war fought partially on colonial behalf. The taxes imposed were light, especially compared to the levies back in England. If the colonies weren't represented in Parliament, neither were most Englishmen; the commonly accepted British doctrine of "virtual representation," which held that every Member of Parliament sat for the Empire as a whole, precluded the need for direct colonial membership. And if the British attempt at instituting a more efficient colonial governance (including a more efficient enforcement of the anti-smuggling laws) seemed oppressive, it was also in accordance with the most advanced doctrines of European mercantile thought. In short, all the British wanted to do was to rationalize, both fiscally and administratively, an Empire which, from London's point of view, desperately needed it.

So what was all the fuss about? What justified the sense of intolerable persecution and imminent doom which the Founding Fathers so frequently invoked as grounds for rebellion? Did the rhetoric simply mask more venal motives? Was the whole affair about indebtedness, commercial restriction, and an unpalatable expansion policy? Did the Founding Fathers really risk death for high treason, or endure an eight-year war, for economic reasons alone? Or was something more involved, something not often made explicit outside the academic study of the period?

In the standard interpretation of the Founding Fathers' political philosophy, the Enlightenment heritage holds pride of place. But whatever the influence of the eighteenth century Enlightenment (and it was great), the Founding Fathers also drew heavily on the old radical Whig canon which their ancestors had brought, and which had survived in America long after it had been generally discarded in England. In this ideology, all questions of government ultimately reduce to the distribution of power: not justice, or opportunity, but power. To the Founding Fathers, power meant only one thing: "the domination of some men over others; the human control of human life: ultimately, physical coercion."[14] Thus, according to Bernard Bailyn, in his classic work, _The Ideological Origins of the American Revolution:_

> The theory of politics . . . [of] the pre-Revolutionary years rest on the belief that what lay behind every political scene, the ultimate explanation of every controversy, was the disposition of power.[15]

To the colonial mind, power was in itself neither good nor bad, merely an ineluctable fact of human life. Human nature, however, possessed an innate tendency toward corruption: a tendency which, in the Whig canon, could signify either the use of power to oppress others _or the abdication of liberties in the face of coercion._ Since power was dynamic, seeking always to expand, and since human beings were doubly corruptible, the solution to this eternal dilemma lay in the institutional diffusion of power. In the radical Whig schema, positive power rested in the Crown and Parliament, with the armed and propertied citizenry acting as a final check on the depredations of either.

At any moment, however, this balance was precarious, dependent upon both prudent government and civic virtue, either or both of which could easily erode or disappear. To the Founding Fathers, men keenly aware of both the British and Greco-Roman pasts, all history taught that this balance could not survive the diminution or loss of any of its components. Surrender civic virtue, or surrender just one liberty, and the whole structure becomes endangered. "All history," writes Gordon Wood, "was therefore an object lesson in the power of the seemingly insignificant."[16] To the Founding Fathers, freedom was an indivisible whole, with no diminution tolerable. No attack on liberties, no matter how small, could be permitted to succeed; one success simply encouraged further depredations. Nor could even potential threats be long endured, and whether that threat came from the British Crown, or even from the mere existence of a strong Continental Army in the midst of a desperate war, no abdication of liberty was thinkable.

But the Founding Fathers were also prudent men, well aware that, even in the easiest of times, the special nature of republican government placed enormous demands upon the human capacity to attain and sustain the necessary virtues. For, in a republic, civic virtue meant not only defense of liberties *in extremis*, but also active participation in public life. Abdication of liberties and refusal to participate in and defend the public life could go hand in hand, just as could abdication of liberties and refusal to oppose the depredations of the state. To the Founding Fathers in the years preceding 1775, it could not but seem that their British brethren had already lost their civic souls by abdicating to the will of centralizing, rationalizing Monarchy and Parliament. Submission to increasing taxation, standing armies, an aggressively expansive Crown and cabals of the "King's Men," putative conspiracies everywhere: Such was the colonial image of the mother country prior to the war. For the Founding Fathers, therefore, revolution entailed more than an attempt to remedy essentially local grievances. It also meant, writes Pocock, "the necessary and triumphant struggle of America to escape from that same [British] corruption."[17] To the Founding Fathers, then, no single item in the "long train of abuses" which Jefferson catalogued in the Declaration of Independence, constituted, in and of itself, *a casus belli*. Nor did they all together. What mattered was their nature as evidence of a plan to reduce the colonies, as Jefferson put it, "under absolute despotism." So sensitive were the Fathers to the nuances of potential oppression that they could not help but see in every Crown enactment, no matter how ostensibly mild or reasonable, the precursor of total tyranny.

And so imbued were the Fathers with this sense of oppressive potential everywhere, *including in each other*, that they chose to risk losing the war rather than endure the perceived perils of large standing armies.

For the Founding Fathers, then, the Revolution entailed far more than the resolution of specific grievances against a specific sovereign; it also embodied the eternal struggle of virtuous men against, not just tyranny, but tyrannical potential. In this struggle, civic virtue failed to motivate the citizenry at large. It failed to man the militias and the army; it failed to fight effectively; it failed to produce any viable middle way between imprudent reliance on the citizenry and equally imprudent reliance on professional warriors. And, in the years after 1783, civic virtue also failed to establish a proper republic. It failed in the rebellions and depredations of the confederal years, in the populistic excesses and inadequacies of the various state governments, and, most of all, in the growing fear that the United States had won its independence from imperial tyranny, only to lose its freedom to ochlocracy and the threat of dissolution at home.

The Founding Fathers solved this problem in 1787. Their solution was both radical and ingenious, a recasting of the republic into the classic Lockean mold. In the old British arrangement, power received its legitimation via a series of *ad hoc* arrangements worked out over centuries. In the old radical Whig schema, the people served, not as the source of power, but as a final check upon it. The American Constitution reversed this arrangement. By locating both the source and the legitimation of power in "We the People," civic virtue became institutionalized in the machinery of government—in the various checks and balances created by the Constitution. By placing the checks and balances within the mechanism, rather than within various social groupings, the Founding Fathers assigned to the machinery the most important functions of civic virtue: the maintenance of balance, the prevention of tyranny, and the providing of the common defense. And nowhere is this new theory of government better exemplified than in the military provisions of the Constitution.

The Constitution of 1787, plus the Bill of Rights and the Militia Act of 1792, codified a new understanding of military claim and service.[18] There would be a small standing professional army, raised and funded by Congress and commanded by the President. It would be used for policing (and expanding) the frontier, defending the arsenals, and as a nucleus for possible wartime expansion, but for little more. The bulk of the nation's military manpower would reside, as before, in the state militias, subject (in theory, at least) to federal oversight. The militias would be available for federal use under specific conditions and for certain emergency purposes: repelling invasion, suppressing insurrection, enforcing federal laws. Universal militia service would still be required, in support of which the Second Amendment decreed that "the right of the people to bear arms shall not be infringed."

In essence, what this complex system sought to achieve was a prudent application of civic virtue to the military needs of a new republic. The necessity of civic virtue remained an article of faith, as did the theoretically compulsory nature of military service. But the federal system required certain institutional changes. As L. D. Cress has described the new arrangement:

> The citizenry retained an obligation to support the military needs of the republic, but that obligation was . . . not the result of public [or civic] virtue. Federalists perceived the military strength of the nation as a consort of special interests, both civil [the federal/state balance] and military, directed by a national government toward a common goal— a goal most efficiently attained through the separate and unique contributions of those interests.[19]

In other words, although civic virtue among the citizenry

remained the *sine qua non* of republican survival, the United States would no longer depend solely upon either the spontaneous manifestation of that virtue, or the ability of the states to compel universal service. Since all power now flowed from the people, civic virtue could be "helped along" by legislation at the federal level, as well as by state enactments and practices, in accordance with the needs and the prudence of the times.

But did this system mandate federal conscription? In theory, enforced military service, at either the state or federal levels, would be no more than a demand made by the people upon itself, and therefore legitimate. But was federal conscription, in 1787, regarded as a proper activity? The answer is, probably yes, although it was neither necessary nor prudent to enact it then, given the lack of foreign military threat and the greater urgency of other issues. The authority to conscript was implicit in the Constitutional settlement—and no doubt more than implicit to the men who had lived through the war. As Alexander Hamilton wrote:

> The authorities essential to the common defense are these: to raise armies; to build and equip fleets; to prescribe rules for the government of both; to direct their operations; to provide for their support. These powers ought to exist without limitation, *because it is impossible to foresee or to define the extent and variety of national exigencies, and the corresponding extent and variety of the means which may be necessary to satisfy them.*[20]
>
> *(The Federalist, #23*, Italics in the original)

True, the Constitution made no explicit mention of conscription, any more than it mentioned abortion, or education, or ecology. Indeed, given the country's physical security at the time, the issue was hardly of paramount importance, and not worth squandering political capital over. Few would have argued forcefully for federal conscription when it was neither immediatley necessary nor proscribed at the state level, and since federalization of the militia constituted a kind of *de facto* conscription in any event.

CONCLUSION

And thus the "original understanding" in the matter of military service:

The responsibility to serve is universal (if only among white males back then).

The bearing of arms is a form, perhaps the highest form, of civic virtue, and constitutes an essential and exemplary demonstration of the citizen's ability to function in the public realm.

This responsibility, though initially derived from a theory of government based upon both British history and radical Whig ideology, changed its form, but not its essence, with the advent of the Constitution.

This required and virtuous service may take different forms, depending upon the circumstances of the times.

It may be compelled, inasmuch as conscription represents a demand made upon the people by itself.

Reliance upon the spontaneous virtue of the citizenry is neither prudent nor safe.

The failure of a free people to "compel itself," when such compulsion is necessary, indicates neither wisdom nor proper regard for individual liberties, but corruption and folly.

In the abstract, this understanding has remained remarkably constant since 1787. But wars are not abstractions, certainly not America's twentieth century wars. Nor is it altogether clear that this understanding can have more relevance to the kinds of wars America is likely to fight for the rest of this century.

Wars such as Vietnam.

Vietnam: The Great Evasion and the Restoration of Ideals

We were just visiting.

Vietnam Veteran in
Al Santoli
Everything We Had

In her classic study, *On Revolution*, Hannah Arendt poses a simple question. Of the three great modern revolutions, the American, French, and Russian, only the American succeeded in establishing the kind of state envisioned by its creators: permanent, humane, and capable of adaptation to the needs of future generations. The French Revolution ended by spawning Napoleon; the Russian Revolution brought forth a brutality and sterility whose final consequences for this planet cannot yet be foreseen. Yet ironically, it has been the two failed revolutions—their putative ideals, their images, their rhetorical and ideological categories—which continue to inspire countless other struggles, while the American accomplishment has remained, in Arendt's evocative phrase, "an event of little more than local importance."[1]

Why should this be?

The answer that Arendt (and numerous other writers) have offered is complex, but may be abstracted as follows: The American Revolution never confronted the extremes of poverty, oppression, and social rigidity found across the rest of the globe. A favorable natural environment, the lack of established aristocracies and churches, a strong pre-revolutionary tradition of self-government, lack of aggressive neighbors, etc., all made it easier. If the American Revolution succeeded, according to this interpretation, it was because most of its work had already been done for it. If it proved to be far more humane than other revolutions, that was because it could afford to be.

It is hard to dispute this contention. Indeed, it is true that most of the American machinery of freedom—elections, civil rights, free speech, civilian control of the military, etc.—has proven non-exportable to the rest of the world. But the Founding Fathers, despite their intense concern with the crafting of such machinery, never assumed that it would be exportable. The ideals and sense of life, yes, the precise techniques, no.

And the Founding Fathers well understood the difficulty even of presenting America as an exemplar to other lands. To quote Arendt:

> As a matter of fact, when the men of the American Revolution came to France and were actually confronted with the social conditions on the continent, with those of the poor as well as of the rich, they no longer believed with Washington that "the American Revolution . . . seems to have opened the eyes of almost every nation in Europe. . . ."
> Some of them, even before, had warned the French officers, who had fought with them in the War of Independence, lest their "hopes be influenced by our triumphs on this virgin soil. You will carry our sentiments with you, but if you try to plant them in a country that has been corrupt for centuries, you will encounter obstacles more formidable than ours. Our liberty has been won with blood; yours will have to be shed in torrents before liberty can take root in the old world."[2]

Thus, the American Revolution might serve as a beacon to others in a world perpetually and habitually oppressed, but neither that Revolution's political techniques nor products could be universally emulated. Nor should American arms be employed in such savage, and usually futile, quests.

Thus the Founding Fathers on the perceived limits of both American power and the American example. And, one might wonder, had the Revolutionary generation somehow returned to earth in April 1975, and watched on television the final helicopters departing from the roof of the American embassy in Saigon, would their reaction have been a collective We Told You So? What might have been the reaction of men who, though fully aware of the uniqueness of their creation, and of the surpassing need to refrain from gratuitous immersion in the miseries of others, also understood political life as the disposition and exercise of power, and tyranny as an eternal, if often ambiguous, enemy? Would they have deemed the Vietnam War an exercise in arrogance, a wholly unnecessary tragedy, or a failure of prudence—of the ability to apply general principles to specific situations? What might they have thought of the civic virtue of those who drew America into the war, of those who fought it, and of those who resisted or evaded it? And what might they have thought of the message now, only now, beginning to be heard from a few American survivors of the political prisons of North Vietnam?

THE "NEW" DEBATE

It is said that something has happened to the American understanding of the Vietnam experience. Something has. It would be surprising if something had not. Ten years or so after the end of any war, the reassessments begin, and Vietnam has proven no exception to that rule. As I write, it is ten years since the fall of Saigon; twenty years since the first Marine landings; thirty years since the United States undertook to supplant the French as guarantor of South Vietnamese sovereignty; forty years since that day in Hanoi when Ho Chi Minh proclaimed the independence of a unified Vietnam, reading from a Declaration of Independence which borrowed whole phrases from the American document, while American officers stood by his side on the outdoor podium and American warplanes flew overhead in salute. It is time, indeed, for the new understanding which is slowly taking shape. It is both necessary and proper that what Norman Podhoretz once referred to as "deliverance from debate"—the post-1975 national silence on the meaning of the tragedy—has given way to a somber, somber, more-in-sorrow, slowly coalescing new view.[3] Certainly, in recent years, both the quality and quantity of Vietnam scholarship has improved: a fact due as much to the release of new material as to the cooling of passions. Certainly, the old continuum of dispute seems to be narrowing. No longer do the professional America-haters enjoy automatic credibility, even among the more ardently disaffected. The simplistic "Vietnam Itself Was the Crime" intepretation, and its ancillary (and no longer possible) glorification of the Marxist enemy, have fallen away. At the other extreme, there has been (mercifully) no "Who Lost Vietnam?" witch hunt, and the "Washington Never Let Us Win" syndrome has been recast in far more complex form. Operating between these two former gospels, the "new" debate, and the recent spate of memoirs, do their quiet work of reckoning.

In reality, however, the "new" debate consists of four separate reappraisals, and though they deal with the same event, neither their methodologies nor their conclusions coincide, nor do the new questions they raise. It is, of course, possible to pick and choose among the four, according to one's personal predilections and professional interests. But only as a sum do they offer the wider perspective so desperately needed, if that ugly time is to be, first understood, then mastered, and then laid to rest.

And only as a sum do these reassessments offer the wider perspective which alone can render military claim and obligation coherent in post-Vietnam America.

The four reassessments are:

1) The decision to intervene. Was it neither altruistic nor evil, but the product of both a fatally flawed American grand strategy and a fatally flawed president?

2) The military conduct of the war itself. Could it have been won? *Was it won?* What does it indicate about theoretical and structural deficiencies in the American manner of war?

3) The conduct of the American people during the war. Why

the self-righteous bizarreness of so much of the anti-war movement, and why the destruction of the concepts of military claim and obligation as legitimate aspects of citizenship?

4) The meaning of defeat.

THE DECISION TO INTERVENE

Even now, it is hard to imagine a place of less intrinsic significance to the United States than Vietnam. Even now, it is hard to overestimate the devastation Vietnam brought to the American anti-Marxist consensus: a policy, a moral sense, shared by this people for nearly a generation. And even now, it continues to be difficult to grasp the complexity of what went wrong. As John Lewis Gaddis has suggested, the Vietnam conundrum consisted of:

> . . . the expansion of means to honor a commitment made as a substitute for means; the justification of that commitment in terms of a balance of power made shaky by its [the commitment's] existence; the defense, in the interests of credibility, of policies destructive of credibility; the search, ultimately, for domestic consensus by means that destroyed that consensus. . . . Indeed, both threats and responses became ends in themselves, with the result that the United States either ignored or forgot what it had set out to do in Vietnam at just the moment it was resolving, with unprecedented determination, to do it.[4]

If this somber description is apt, it means that Vietnam was, first and foremost, *a failure of mind*: a failure of thoughtlessness on a truly historic scale: a triumph made possible by a mindless American geopolitical strategy, containment, and by an American president's equally mindless determination to remake the country in his own image, and be worshipped for it thereby.

To consider the larger, the geopolitical, failure first:

It is historically convenient (although hardly precise) to assign the same birthday to both the Cold War and to the American strategy for waging it: March 12, 1947. On that day, Harry Truman announced to a joint session of Congress that:

> I believe it must be the policy of the United States to support free peoples who are resisting attempted subjugation by armed minorities or by outside influences.[5]

Specifically, the Truman Doctrine (as it came to be known) applied to Greece and Turkey, then under threat of Marxist domination—the former due to a civil war, the latter due to Soviet pressure. Clearly, Truman never intended to extend a blank check to the rest of the non-Marxist planet. However, almost immediately, and certainly with the advent of Korea, the doctrine acquired a global relevance. Henceforward, the United States would undertake to oppose armed Marxism around the world.

If the Truman Doctrine provided the most succinct statement of post-World War II American foreign policy, that policy's working vocabulary came from several other sources. Taken together, these comprise what might be called the "canon of containment"—America's theoretical justification, and grand strategy, *vis-à-vis* both Soviet power and global armed Marxism. These other sources were two documents by George Kennan, his "Long Telegram" from Moscow in 1946 and his 1947 *Foreign Affairs* article, "The Sources of Soviet Conduct," plus a 1949 National Security Council paper, which came to be known as NSC-68. The first two documents purported to explain Soviet motivations and behavior; the third, approved by Truman in 1950 but not declassified until 1974, set forth the rationale for massive peacetime rearmament and sustained global interventionism. Although these three documents contain a number of differences, they do form a canonical whole: the world-view of American foreign policy, and of American global purpose, from Harry Truman to Ronald Reagan (with a brief hiatus under Jimmy Carter). Obviously, many more forces than anti-Marxism and fear of Soviet power helped shape American foreign policy during this period. But rarely have the essentials of national purpose been so clearly delineated.

In essence, the canon of containment has four parts: an assessment of Soviet motivations, an analysis of Soviet conduct, a recommended response, and a statement of the consequences of failure to respond.

To take them in turn:

According to the canon, Soviet behavior finds its motivations in an array of sources, ranging from traditional Russian xenophobia and expansionism, through Marxist-Leninist ideology, to the ongoing need of the ruling hierarchy to justify repression, privation, and terror at home by cultivating a sense of foreign threat. Taken together, these heuristics and needs produce a highly distorted view of the non-Marxist world: a set of erroneous, albeit highly useful, misperceptions. As Kennan wrote in his "Long Telegram," sent from Moscow while he served in the U.S. embassy as *chargé d'affaires:*

> At bottom of Kremlin's neurotic view of world affairs is instinctive Russian sense of insecurity. . . . Marxist dogma . . . became perfect vehicle for sense of insecurity. . . . Today they cannot dispense with it. It is their fig leaf of respectability. Without it they would stand before history, at best, as only the last of that long succession of cruel and wasteful Russian rulers . . .[6]

Further, according to Kennan:

> . . . the stress laid in Moscow on the menace confronting

Soviet security from the world outside its borders is founded not in the realities of foreign antagonism but in the necessity of explaining away the maintenance of dictatorial authority at home.[7]

Thus, ran the canon, the confluence of Russian history, aggressive and millennarian ideology, and domestic politics produced a government almost incapable of rational perception of the world. Not insane: far from it, but inextricably enmeshed in a web of mutually reinforcing distortions which had proven too useful to relinquish. Moreover, from the Soviet point of view, this perceived danger had to be total, since their own intents (according to the canon) were also uncompromisingly aggressive. Concluded NSC-68:

. . . the Soviet Union, unlike previous aspirants to [world] hegemony, is animated by a new fanatic faith antithetical to our own, and seeks to impose its absolute authority on the rest of the world. Conflict has therefore become endemic and is waged, on the part of the Soviet Union, by violent and non-violent methods, in accordance with the dictates of expediency. . . .

The design, therefore, calls for the complete subversion or forcible destruction of the machinery of government and the structure of society in the countries of the non-Soviet world.[8]

If Soviet conduct flowed logically from irrational (by Western standards) Soviet perceptions and from an abhorrent totalitarian ideology, the character of such behavior could then reasonably be predicted. If conflict was required, whether for ideological, geostrategic, or domestic political reasons, the Soviet oligarchy would generate such conflict, *regardless of Western capability or intent.* And since such perpetual conflict, carefully managed, served an array of Soviet interests, no respite could be expected. Indeed, none was possible, for American attempts to deal with the Soviet Union as a normal power would prove not only fruitless, but also irrelevant. To be sure, the Soviet Union, a power in no hurry to achieve Marxism's inevitable triumph, and also a power too cautious to endanger itself irrevocably, might on occasion negotiate or yield on specific issues. But the overall pattern of Soviet conduct, according to the canon, would remain belligerent. Not apocalyptically so, but belligerent nonetheless.

To what extent did this assessment correspond to the actual realities of either Soviet power or Stalin's intents? To what extent was it actually a set of interlocking self-delusions mirroring those which the Soviets were perceived as holding? It is, of course, impossible to know. However, in the latter 1940's, was it really logical to conclude that the Soviet Union, still prostrate from twenty years of purges and war, still engaged in the absorption of its newly acquired East European empire, could have posed a serious military threat to anybody? Might it not have been more prudent to assume that the bellicose aura emanating from Moscow, and the savage repressions in the satellite states, constituted proof more of nervous weakness than of confident strength? Analysts such as Adam Ulam have plausibly argued that it was America's sense of its own military weakness, a weakness self-imposed by the rapid postwar demobilization, which caused the Soviet threat to appear far more ominous than it really was.[9] It is also plausible that concern over Europe's slow postwar recovery, plus the deteriorating situation in China, led policy-makers to adopt a "worst-case scenario" regarding Soviet intentions, even at the expense of a realistic estimate of Soviet capabilities (which may or may not have been available at the time).

Ironically, this gloomy assessment engendered neither defeatism nor despair. In fact, it generated quite the opposite among the authors of the canon; it produced both optimism and a new sense of purpose. The canon held that, although the Kremlin required world tension for both domestic and ideological reasons, and fully expected to achieve world domination, it did not appear bent on conquest in any Hitlerian way. Indeed, according to the canon, Moscow's faith in Marxism's inevitable triumph actually served to restrain rash adventurism. Low-grade, protracted conflict would probably be the norm. And low-grade, protracted conflict could be met. In the crucial passage of the whole canon, Kennan wrote:

> . . . Soviet pressure against the free institutions of the Western world is something that can be *contained* by the adroit and vigilant application of counterforce at a series of constantly shifting geographical and political points, corresponding to the shifts and maneuvers of Soviet policy . . .[10] (Italics added)

The central notion of containment thus held that the threat could be neutralized by meeting it whenever and wherever it appeared. Or, to put it another way: Since the Russians, when confronted by a firm show of resolve, would probably back off and try somewhere else (one crisis being as useful as another), it stood to reason that a series of successful containings would save the non-Marxist world. No cataclysmic escalations would be necessary (although the threat might occasionally be useful). All that would be needed was the ability to demonstrate firmness, plus an occasional willingness to back it up with a little muscle. And, reasoned Kennan (who subsequently disavowed the whole doctrine), the process need not continue forever. Eventually, he argued, most likely within twenty years, the Soviet oligarchy would grow weary of the struggle, or perhaps be transformed from within by the successor generation.[11] In the interim, however, failure to achieve a series of successful containings could have irreversible consequences. Avowed NSC-68, the secret document which recommended massive American rearmament in 1949:

> The risks we face are of a new order of magnitude, com-

mensurate with the total struggle in which we are engaged. For a free society there is never total victory, since freedom and democracy are never wholly attained, are always in the process of being attained. But defeat at the hands of the totalitarians is total defeat.[12]

Containment, then, was theory, method, goal, and call to rearmament. The theory proposed that Soviet expansionism responded to unique Soviet needs, that it ran on its own imperatives, and that it could not be handled with the normal tools of diplomacy and international affairs. The method involved opposition to Soviet and Soviet-backed expansionism; no serious thought was given to liberation of areas already under Soviet control (although the rhetoric of "rollback" permeated the Eisenhower administration). The goal was to hasten the "mellowing" of Soviet conduct by demonstrating its futility over a long period of years. Finally, the canon concluded with an affirmation of the moral rightness of this course of action. Avowed Kennan, in a passage which now must seem both hubristic and bizarre:

> Surely there was never a fairer test of national quality than this. In the light of these circumstances, the thoughtful observer of Russian-American relations will find no cause for complaint in the Kremlin's challenge to American society. He will rather experience a certain gratitude to a Providence which, by providing the American people with an implacable challenge, has made their entire security as a nation dependent on their pulling together and accepting the responsibilities of moral and political leadership that history plainly intended them to bear.[13]

In a certain sense, containment was a doctrine with which the Founding Fathers might have had a certain sympathy. Their sense of politics had been identical, their belief that freedom constitutes an indivisible whole, that any surrender to oppression could well endanger the whole. Their sense of

America as the last best hope of man might also have led them to approve of containment. And, even though the Founding Fathers constantly warned against foreign involvements, their warnings made more sense in the eighteenth century than in the twentieth.

All in all, then, the Founding Fathers might have seen containment as the application of American civic virtue on a global scale: an application, and a scale, made necessary by the realities of twentieth century life.

But they would have, I suspect, found containment utterly lacking in prudential wisdom: in the ability to apply general principles to specific situations. And they would probably have found it imprudent for three basic reasons.

First, containment violated a cardinal principle of the strategic art: *retain the initiative.* An essentially reactive strategy, containment from its inception condemned the United States to a mindlessly reflexive stance. All America could do was careen from crisis to crisis, sometimes successfully, sometimes not, always more driven by events (and by the vagaries of public opinion) than by any coherently pursued grand strategy. Despite some initial (and enduring) successes, it soon became apparent that containment, by its abdication of initiative, reduced the United States to mere reactivity—a sure prescription for gradual exhaustion.

But reactivity *per se* would not have been so disastrous, had it not been for a second, perhaps even greater failure in prudence. For containment exemplified the truth of another principle of the strategic art: *he who tries to defend everywhere, ends up defending nowhere.* To be sure, opposition to armed Marxism is in no moral sense wrong, but the United States never possessed (and does not now possess) the resources to defend the entire non-Marxist world. In fairness, it must be pointed out that neither Kennan's formulation nor the Truman Doctrine were meant to be promiscuously globalized;

Kennan considered only the defense of the industrialized west, Japan, and the Western Hemisphere vital, while the Truman Doctrine initially applied only to Greece and Turkey. But promiscuous globalization was inherent in the canon: a globalization made official by the American intervention in Korea, a place which both the Truman administration and the Joint Chiefs of Staff had decreed nonessential only weeks before the war began. What Truman started, Eisenhower would continue: the extension of American guarantees, via over seventy treaties and bilateral agreements, to almost the entire non-Marxist planet. The logic of globalization seemed clear enough to the authors of NSC-68:

> . . . in the context of the present polarization of power, a defeat for free institutions *anywhere* is a defeat *everywhere*.[14]

In some metaphysical sense, this was no doubt the case. And, of course, every defeat entails unpleasant consequences. Prudence, however, dictates, that not every loss, or potential loss, be endowed *by the losers* with apocalyptic significance. And thus the third of containment's prudential errors: It magnified the real-world dangers of even peripheral defeats, and vastly enlarged the scope of perceived American vital interests. As John Lewis Gaddis has written:

> From this perspective, changes in the balance of power could occur, not only as a result of economic maneuvers or military action, but from intimidation, humiliation, or even loss of credibility.[15]

Or, as Lyndon Johnson would write in his memoirs, explaining his decision to intervene in the Vietnam War:

> Dean Rusk expressed one worry that was much on my mind. It lay at the heart of our Vietnam policy. "If the Com-

munist world finds out that we will not pursue our commitments to the end," he said, "I don't know where they will
stay their hand."

I felt sure they would *not* stay their hand. If we ran out
on Southeast Asia, I could see trouble ahead in every part
of the globe—not just in Asia but the Middle East and in
Europe, in Africa and Latin America. I was convinced that
our retreat from this challenge would open the path to
World War III.[16]

Here the canon of containment finds its imprudent, illogical,
and indeed absurd fruition: the belief that any failure, anywhere, must inevitably lead to either Armageddon or a Marxist planet: the belief that, regardless of the realities and complexities of world history, or of the Marxist movement itself, or
of common sense, an ugly little war in a place that Johnson
himself often described as a "pissant country" could determine the fate of the world . . . *because we said it could.*

But did Johnson really believe it?

In part, no doubt: Lyndon Johnson partook fully of both the
metaphysics of containment, and also of the "Munich syndrome" so much on the minds of his predecessors. No doubt,
also, more than a trace of machismo and ego were involved;
he surely meant it when he declared, loudly and often, that he
would not be the first American president to lose a war. But
whatever his foreign concerns, Lyndon Johnson was primarily
a domestic politician, whose major ambition was massive social engineering, and who desired to be remembered (and
loved) as the architect of the Great Society. He could not help
but view Vietnam within the context of domestic politics, specifically the maintenance of the Congressional support necessary to enact his programs. In his own lifetime, he had seen
the reforms of Franklin Roosevelt vitiated and those of Harry
Truman aborted by war. Once the shooting began, all Congressional impetus to domestic reform died, and often such re-

forms as had been achieved were quietly dismantled by the entrenched Republican-conservative Democratic alliance. Johnson knew that war in Vietnam, win or lose, would probably destroy his domestic agenda. In a now famous conversation with Doris Kearns, he claimed:

> "I knew from the start . . . that I was bound to be crucified either way I moved. If I left the woman I really loved— the Great Society—in order to get involved with that bitch of a war on the other side of the world, then I would lose everything at home. All my programs. All my hopes to feed the hungry and shelter the homeless. All my dreams to provide education and medical care to the browns and the blacks and the lame and the poor. But if I left the war and let the Communists take over South Vietnam, then I would be seen as a coward and my nation would be seen as an appeaser. . . .
>
> Oh, I could see it coming all right. History provided too many cases where the sound of the bugle put an immediate end to the hopes and dreams of the best reformers . . . because the war had to come first.[17]

No doubt, Lyndon Johnson (speaking in retrospect and for posterity) meant what he said. But, in recent years, a new consensus has begun to emerge concerning the relative weighting of Mr. Johnson's foreign and domestic concerns during the crucial months of 1964 and 1965. To be sure, no one can really know what went on in Johnson's mind. But it now seems clear that all the highly publicized "crisis meetings," all the now-declassified memoranda, even the presence of the resident Cassandra, George Ball, served less to discuss and work out realistic options than to legitimize a decision which Johnson had already taken.

That decision was: to commit American forces to warfare on the Asian mainland in order to *buy time to enact his domestic agenda*. If this is true, then America went to war in Vietnam, not just because of the obsession with containment, but

also for the sake of day care centers in Philadelphia, urban re-
newal in Harlem, adult literacy classes in Mississippi, and all
the rest of Lyndon Johnson's social engineering schemes. If
this is true, then it surely must constitute one of the most bizarre linkages in world history, and one of the most tragic.

The facts are these.

When Lyndon Jonson succeeded to the Presidency, he in-
herited a commitment of 16,000 Americans in-country (already actively participating in combat), a Saigon government
in post-Diem chaos, and an ever-increasing possibility, not of
outright defeat, but of a South Vietnamese government compelled to seek terms. Between November 1963, when the
problem became Johnson's, and July 1965, when he ordered
200,000 combat and support troops to Vietnam, he never
consulted the American people. Incessantly, he claimed that
the United States neither desired to fight in Vietnam nor
would escalate. Johnson presented every escalation as "no
departure" from this policy. Each step in that escalation—the
Tonkin Gulf retaliation of 1964, the Rolling Thunder bombing
campaign, the Marine landing at Da Nang to guard the air
field, the change in the Marine mission to permit aggressive
patrolling, then full commitment—each was downplayed, presented low-key (often at press conferences), and touted as "no
change in policy."

Yet, as he escalated, never did he even come close to au-
thorizing the military measures which might have brought the
war, if not to victory, then to a satisfactory conclusion. Consistently, Johnson chose to do the minimum necessary to prevent *short-term* defeat: to stave off disaster while his domestic
program was still wending through Congress. Never did Johnson authorize, or even propose, the appropriate war-time
measures: mobilization of reserves, tax increases, and, most of
all, a declaration of war.

But Lyndon Johnson, it is now clear, was not deceived by

anyone into believing that the escalations he authorized might end the war. No responsible senior military adviser ever suggested that the war could be won easily or, given the restraints imposed, won at all. Indeed, whenever Johnson consulted with his Joint Chiefs of Staff, he seemed more interested in asking them, "What can you do with what I'm giving you?" than "Should we be doing this at all?" Lyndon Johnson did not stumble blindly into Vietnam, misled by his generals. Instead, he chose to create, he sanctioned the creation, of what Daniel Ellsberg has aptly labelled the "stalemate machine"— a megalith designed not to attain victory, but to buy time at an ever-increasing cost in lives, treasure, and political support.[18]

That he was able to make these decisions, military choices which no competent corporal would have made, was due in part to the sterility of containment. It was also due to his domestic concerns. But, were his decisions simply the product of mindlessness, or of Machiavellian calculation, the disaster would not have been so great. Tragically, however, Lyndon Johnson was able to evade the full implications of his choices by relying on a theory of war-making every bit as absurd and pernicious as the notion of global containment: the theory of so-called "limited war."

THE CONDUCT OF THE WAR

In the final days of April 1975, U. S. Army Colonel Harry Summers found himself in Hanoi, a member of the American delegation charged with supervising the 1973 Paris peace accords. Unfortunately, the final North Vietnamese offensive, then in progress, had left him somewhat underemployed. While waiting for Saigon to fall, one of Colonel Summers' North Vietnamese counterparts attempted to console him. In an act of military courtesy, the North Vietnamese officer suggested that Colonel Summers should not feel too badly; after all, the Americans had done everything they could. Colonel Summers replied that the United States had never suffered a single major defeat in the field. There had been losses, there had been reversals, but never a significant defeat. True, replied the North Vietnamese officer: but not relevant.[19]

Why not? What was it that made for this "irrelevance of victory"? Or, to ask it another way, why did seven years of nearly continuous American battlefield *success* make no final difference?

It has often been argued that the Vietnam War was unwinable: that all the enemy had to do was survive until the United States grew weary and left. It has also been pointed out *ad infinitum* that a totally committed small power, fighting on its own territory, can usually prevail over a major power with ambiguous commitment, especially when that small power employs totalitarian methods of population mobilization and control. Finally it has been noted *ad nauseam* that no American administration ever attempted to engage domestic public opinion on any significant scale, often for alleged fear of engendering an uncontrollable hyper-enthusiasm. Certainly, Lyndon Johnson feared war hysteria as one more threat to his beloved Great Society; perhaps he feared it as much as defeat in Vietnam. All these points have their merits. But the ironic fact remains: The failure of the war was not military, but intellectual. *Victory was not to be had primarily because it was never sought. All the battlefield successes, and the successes of such paramilitary programs as Phoenix and CORDS, availed for nothing because Washington operated under a theory of war which made combat itself irrelevant.*

Could America have won in Vietnam? The answer is, we probably did, and never knew it. As military analysts such as Colonel Summers and General Bruce Palmer have pointed out, American forces in Vietnam did everything that was asked of them. The problem was: They were asked to do the wrong things. And they were asked to do the wrong things be- cause, according to the then-fashionable theory of limited war, it didn't matter what they were asked to do. Lyndon Johnson did not opt for escalating stalemate simply because the Ameri- can military wasn't capable of anything more. Nor did he opt for it solely to buy a few crucial months for his Great Society. He could choose it because of the influence of a theory of con- flict which held that a policy of deliberate non-victory could lead to satisfactory results.

As already noted, the canon of containment, an essentially defensive, reactive, static strategy, aimed for the maintenance of a global status quo. Since military force was only one tool among many, it alone was not expected to achieve decisive results, especially given the legitimate fear of Soviet nuclear weapons and Chinese hordes. On the surface, this would seem both logical and prudent, and a sensible acknowledgement of Clausewitz' dictum that war is politics by other means. Ob- viously, military power and other tools must be co-ordinated to achieve successful policy. But in the 1950's, with a number of influential academic theorists taking the lead, this military/ non-military equation was recast in an historically unprece- dented manner. Much of this recasting came out of the emerg- ing study of nuclear strategy.[20] Much of it centered on the problems of keeping limited wars from escalating into nuclear exchange. But when it came to be applied to the conduct of conventional and subconventional war *per se*, the result was a set of self-delusions and misperceptions fully as pernicious as containment itself.

Throughout history, most wars have been limited in both scope and intensity. Total war appears to be the prerogative of the very primitive and very advanced. But, historically, lim- ited wars have been *fought*: Military objectives were specific, and the attainment of battlefield success (or lack thereof) dic- tated the effectiveness of diplomacy in most cases.

The new theory of limited war, however, did away with this old relationship. In this theory, force and threat of force were to be used primarily as means of communicating with the adversary, not as means of victory in their own right. Once we had (to borrow the jargon) "signalled our determination," a rational (by western, non-Marxist standards) adversary would either negotiate or withdraw. Failing this outcome, American force would be employed in tightly calibrated increments, until such time as the enemy "got the message." Or, as General Maxwell Taylor (one of President Kennedy's chief advisers) told a Senate hearing: The United States was not trying to defeat North Vietnam, only "to cause them to mend their ways."[21]

In a Vietnam-type situation, with few pieces of critical terrain, practically no really lucrative bombing targets, and with the ever-present (although, in retrospect, vastly overrated) threat of Chinese or Soviet intervention, the use of force became largely "communicative." Where we bombed mattered less than demonstrating our willingness to bomb. Where the search-and-destroy operations took place mattered less than that they happened. Further, given Johnson's obsession for personal target and weapon selection, and McNamara's penchant for reducing battlefield reality to statistical indices, it became inevitable that actual combat would devolve into a *melange* whose primary purpose was, as Hendrik Hertzberg put it, to demonstrate "our will to demonstrate our will."[22]

Ironically, however, an enemy who could not be "communicated with"—who simply got the message and then kept on coming—was very nearly defeated on the battlefield.[23] Only now is it becoming apparent just how badly decimated the North Vietnamese were, how close to extinction the Viet Cong came after Tet, and how devastatingly effective both American arms and counter-insurgency programs could be. But Washington, equating success with dubious statistics and "positive feedback" from Hanoi, never saw the reality. Nor did the media, nor the people at large.

In sum, a generation before Vietnam, the United States embarked upon a grand strategy, containment, which, although originally conceived as a transitory expedient, became first institutionalized, then globalized, then coupled with a doctrine of limited war which deemed combat an exercise in management and communication. Under the canon of containment, stalemate was the desired, indeed the best possible outcome in any encounter; with the doctrine of limited war, it could (theoretically) be had without undue concern for battlefield realities or public opinion. No more efficacious formula for defeat at the hands of a totally-committed adversary could have been found.

Still, could the war have really been won? Could American military force, properly applied, have gained at least a long-term remission in the South, if not the actual conquest of the North? In his study of the war, *On Strategy*, Colonel Summers suggests that, had the United States used its forces to seal off South Vietnam from North Vietnamese infiltration and resupply (a task which would have included occupation of parts of Laos, Cambodia, and North Vietnam, plus the sealing of Haiphong Harbor), coupled with a full-scale air campaign in the north, while letting the South Vietnamese deal with the insurgency, a reasonable victory might have been obtained.

Would such a strategy have worked, given the limitations of the Saigon government and the various pressures upon Lyndon Johnson?

We'll never know.

THE CONDUCT OF THE PEOPLE

Henry Kissinger once remarked that almost anything one

might care to say about the Vietnam War would be at least partially true. If this be so for the fighting itself, and for the strategies (or lack thereof) which determined its peculiar nature, how much more must it be true for the conduct of the American people during this time. Even now, it is still impossible to sort out the myriad responses, and the emotions and purposes which formed and impelled them. No conclusion enjoys, or can enjoy, indisputable validity; no perception can be proven true. Having said this, I should like to offer two conclusions and one perception concerning the conduct of the American people during the Vietnam era.

First, the American people never supported the Vietnam War, *as that war was conducted.*

Second, there never was an organized mass opposition to the war, *as such oppositions have traditionally been formed and implemented.*

Third, although the anti-war movement contained its share of traditional pacifists, genuine (and heroic) resisters, self-interested young men and women, and bizarre hangers-on, none of them gave the movement its unique character—a character which, I shall suggest in a moment, represents the antithesis of political discourse and life, as politics has been known since Aristotle.

To take them in turn:

First, the American people never supported the Vietnam War, as that war was conducted. Rather, as the conflict evolved through what Paul Kattenberg has aptly labelled its two phases of "winning without winning" and "losing without losing," the American people extended the benefit of the doubt to their leaders . . . extended it for far too long.[24] Since the American people were never asked, either directly or through their elected representatives, to consent in the only way that matters constitutionally, through a declaration of war, the question of support became primarily statistical. In

American political discourse, opinion polls came to play the same bizarre role that body counts did in Vietnam: manipulable, often meaningless indices of success or failure. Yet the polls tell a rather odd story. Not until 1971, after Tet, after Cambodia, after Kent State, after half a decade of protest, did a majority of Americans come to favor rapid withdrawal: which was, of course, by then Nixon's policy.[25] Further, in the years preceding 1971, a negative response to the question "Do you approve of the way Mr. Johnson (or Mr. Nixon) is handling the war?" more often indicated desire for victory than withdrawal. This desire for more aggressive prosecution could often express itself in unusual ways. A survey taken among New Hampshire Democrats two days after Eugene McCarthy's great "anti-war" primary victory indicated that over half the voters didn't know he was a dove, and the more they learned about his position, the less likely they were to vote for him.[26] Nor did the media seem able to effect massive changes in public opinion; during the 1968 Tet offensive, now commonly portrayed as the war's great divide, public support for the war effort actually went up.

Clearly, then, the American people tolerated the war until the last vestiges of perceived purpose fell away, and the damage being done to the country *by both the war and the opposition to that war*, became insupportable.

But if it be true that the vast majority of Americans simply tolerated, rather than actively supported, the war, why was it able to drag on so long? Why was the anti-war movement unable to stop it? Why, as Nancy Zaroulis put it in her encomium to the resistance, *Who Spoke Up?* was it that ". . . you could mount an insurgent movement, you could topple a sitting President, you could even deny the presidency to an offending party. What you could not do—what no one seemed to be able to do—was stop the war."[27]

In part, this was no doubt due to the institutional cowardice of the other two branches of government, the Congress and the Supreme Court, both of which had the power to end the war: the former by refusing to appropriate money, the latter by ruling on its constitutionality. In part, also, this was due to the never-clearly-articulated, and constantly changing, sets of objectives issued by various administrations. From stopping monolithic communism to getting back our POW's, the American people were treated to a virtual smorgasbord of war aims, any one of which could seem at least minimally plausible at the time. And, ultimately, the final war aim resembled the first. As Hannah Arendt has written:

> It is indeed true that American policy pursued no real aims, good or bad, that could limit and control sheer fantasy. . . .
> The ultimate aim was neither power nor profit. Nor was it even influence in the world in order to serve particular, tangible interests for the sake of which prestige, an image of the "greatest power in the world," was needed and purposefully used. The goal was now the image itself . . .[28]

At the Washington level, perhaps. At the level of the American people, unaccustomed to defeat and used to self-respect, perhaps. But was this nebulous array of aims, coupled with a national unwillingness to admit a costly mistake, the real source of the anti-war movement's frustration?

Or, to ask it another way, was this frustration what drove large segments of the movement to assume the forms it did: that of a carnival superimposed upon a tragedy, of nihilistic lunacy, of mere self-indulgence?

It would be both unfair and overly simplistic to equate the anti-war movement with its more demented fringes, just as it would be inaccurate to impute lofty motivations to its entire membership. The movement contained its share of serious pacifists, men and women (often middle-aged or older) for whom Vietnam was just one more battle in a lifetime of struggle. The movement also contained its share of young men driven to resistance for reasons of genuine morality, although it might be noted that, of 26,800,000 men who came of draft age during the Vietnam era, only 3,250 were imprisoned for draft offenses of any kind, and that most of these were paroled within a year.[29] Given the Supreme Court's redefinition of conscience, the length of the appeals process, the cumbersome nature of the Selective Service System, and the fact that only a small percentage of the baby boom generation was even needed to fight the war, evasion masquerading as resistance was probably more the norm than high morality. Further, the anti-war movement was never a homogenous entity; it contained numerous organizations and sects for whom Vietnam was less a critical issue than a means to effect other changes in American society. As Thomas Powers has written:

> Opponents of the war found it always difficult, and often impossible, to agree on the best way of opposing it. One reason for this dissension was the fact that the war was actually a secondary issue to many of the organizations most active in trying to end it. The dozen or so minor socialist and revolutionary groups in the United States made no secret of their primary interest in bringing down capitalism. The civil rights organizations were more concerned with injustice at home than war abroad. Student groups were worried about the draft, and were especially prone to bruising ideological struggles on points of purely theoretical interest. Traditional organizations like SANE and Americans for Democratic Action were obsessed with being "responsible" . . .[30]

All true, no doubt. But even conceding these points, it must still be asked: Why did so much of the anti-war movement take the form that it did—less a political than a cultural, social, sexual, and, above all else, psychological affair? Why was so much of it a spasm, a tantrum, an exercise in radical chic and self-gratification for which the war provided less a political cause than an excuse for doing one's own thing. Recent writers on the anti-war movement, such as Nancy Zaroulis, have tended to dismiss this aspect as "little adolescent gestures of rebellion" usually embarrassing to the "adult wing of the movement."[31] But the practitioners of those little gestures—such as carrying Viet Cong and North Vietnamese flags, trashing universities, committing crimes—are now adults, many nearly middle-aged. What they did cannot be dismissed as mere immaturity, for, I think, it presaged a new kind of psychological politics in this country: a politics which this country should never have tolerated and which it cannot now afford.

In an evocative work published in 1983, *America's Quest for the Ideal Self*, social critic Peter Clecak offered a simple postulate.[32] According to Clecak, the quest for self-fulfillment has become the *leitmotif* of American culture, and political dissent one more aspect of self-fulfillment. In Clecak's schema, what one dissents about matters less than that one avail oneself of the potentialities for "growth" and "fulfillment" available in such activities. If Vietnam ceases to gratify, there's a whole catalogue of causes available: whales, snail darters, nuclear freezes, apartheid. None holds any binding claim. Thus, Clecak argues, there was no essential discontinuity between the Sixties, Seventies, and Eighties; the causes varied, the motivations and purposes did not.

Can this be true? Can it be, as Clecak suggests, that sometime during the Vietnam War, politics ceased to be the conduct of the public business, the brokerage of stable competing interests, the quest for objective forms of justice, and became —especially for large segments of America's most privileged youth—simply another form of self-expression and self-gratification? How odd it now seems to read the reasons people gave back then for their activism. A few samples, chosen almost at random from the confessions of self-styled resisters:

> The politics came after the people. There was always a
> personal relationship first. And the most important thing of
> what you were going to do with a person was personal, not
> political.

And:

> It was only when I first began to do my first political activ-
> ity, which was—I can't remember, a boycott or something
> —but I really started to move personally.

And:

> I sort of feel myself to be open [in the resistance] and I
> feel very happy. It is like I have built myself a whole new
> world.[33]

And:

> The most important thing was the feeling of community
> with the people with whom I did it. . . .
> It died for me when the great people like Henry, Bob,
> Rick, and Irene did not come back in the fall [of 1968], and
> when they left for other things I began to lose interest. . . .
> The loss of identity was rather painful.[34]

And how odd it now seems that an ostensibly anti-war
movement should partake so freely of the sexual. Historically,
war releases sexual passions' historically, the major male ben-
eficiaries of this release have been the warriors. Not so Vietnam, with its confluence of feminism and war protest and its
campus rally slogan, "Girls Say Yes to Guys Who Say No,"
and its ancillary *carte blanche* (for those so inclined) to use the
justifications of feminism and anti-war sentiment as excuse to
insult, degrade, and attack those in uniform, especially Vietnam veterans. How much, I wonder, of the ERA's ultimate
demise was due, not to mere "macho backlash," but to the fa-
tigued indifference of men no longer willing to acquiesce in the
demands of their former tormenters.

And how odd it now seems that so much of the anti-war movement should have partaken so freely of the offensive, the bizarre, the trendy, the chic, the snobbish. In 1966, writes Zaroulis:

> . . . resistance to the draft took a new turn. Barry Bondhus, a young draft-eligible Minnesotan from the town of Big Lake, broke into his local draft board and mutilated hundreds of 1-A draft records. His action was remarkable for more than the fact that it was the first of the draft board raids that would reach to near-epidemic numbers by 1969. Bondhus defiled, so to speak, the record by pouring over them two large buckets of human feces. . . . Big Lake One, as the Bondhus action came to be known, was celebrated as "the movement that started the Movement."[35]

The following year, Norman Mailer attended the first march on the Pentagon. Invited to speak at a rally, he recorded in *The Armies of the Night*: "There was a party first, however, given by an attractive liberal couple."[36] Plans for ending the war included:

> A thousand children will stage Loot-Ins at department stores to strike at the property fetish that underlies genocidal war. As the cameras wheel in for the classic counter-demonstration footage, the BOMB PEKING signs will be flipped away to say, "Does LBJ Suck?" During a block party in front of the White House a lad of nine will climb the fence and piss, piss . . .[37]

And how amusing it might seem, were it not for the kind of incident recorded three years later by paraplegic veteran Ron Kovic:

> We went back to the rally for a while, then went on down to the Reflecting Pool. Hundreds of people had taken off their clothes. . . . I didn't know what all of this had to do with the invasion of Cambodia or the students slain at Kent State, but it was total freedom.[38]

Total freedom? For a man condemned to spend his life in a wheel chair, perhaps. But for the country which endured both the war and the anti-universe of radical chic, adolescent tantrum, sexual anarchy, pharmacological excess, moral flatulence, and self-interest masquerading as high moral principle —for the country which has, finally, begun to come to terms with what happened—perhaps it would not be too much to suggest that any list of "lessons of Vietnam" must include those pertaining to the resistance, as well as those of the war itself.

THE LESSONS OF VIETNAM

It is easy to speak of the lessons of Vietnam; hundreds are lying around. A sample might include:

— The intellectual and geopolitical bankruptcy of promiscuously globalized containment as the highest expression of American purpose and policy.

— The objective limits of American power.

— The impossiblity of prosecuting war successfully without the prior and overwhelming support of the American people, a support properly expressed in a declaration of war, not in the weekly printouts of professional survey takers and media pundits.

— The impossibility of managing war, or using combat as "communication." War must be fought, not played according to game theory or business theory or whatever.

— The dangers inherent in permitting extremists or crazies to seize the moral high ground in time of war.

The list could, of course, go on, and even include some opposite conclusions. Rather than do so, however, it might be more useful to conclude with a lesson which has not yet really been made explicit: the importance of individual and national honor, not just as moral luxury, but as the *sine qua non* of this nation's, and perhaps this planet's, survival. In his valuable study of Vietnam veterans, *Home from the War*, the activist psychiatrist Robert Jay Lifton defined Vietnam as a "counterfeit universe"—a place where neither warrior grandeur nor meaningful accomplishment were possible.[39] If Lifton is correct, then what made the experience so traumatic for so many was not the horror *per se*, but the inability of any individual self-respect to survive it. Lifton wrote in the early 1970's; the emergence of the Vietnam veteran over the past few years has demonstrated that he was not entirely correct. But his notion of the "counterfeit universe" should not be dismissed, for if Vietnam was indeed a counterfeit, were there not also two others, one in Washington D.C. and one among large segments of the anti-war movement? Perhaps the Washington counterfeit no longer exists; if it does not, then "Vietnam Syndrome" may be reckoned a positive force, and "No More Vietnams" wise counsel indeed. And perhaps the more honest among the war evaders have begun to face themselves. In an essay written some years ago, James Fallows (Harvard, Rhodes Scholar, now an editor of the *Atlantic*) remarked how convenient it was that the morally correct course of action, draft evasion, kept the evaders alive, out of jail, and free to pursue their educations and careers. Fallows recounted his own experience as a Harvard senior, faking psychological disability at his induction physical while the young men from South Boston went to war:

> I walked in a trance . . . until the final meeting with the fatherly physician who ruled on marginal cases such as mine. I stood there in socks and underwear, arms wrapped

around me in the chilly building. I knew as I looked at the doctor's face that he understood exactly what I was doing.

"Have you ever contemplated suicide?" he asked after he finished looking over my chart. My eyes darted up to his. "Oh, suicide—yes, I've been feeling very unstable and unreliable recently." He looked at me, staring until I returned my eyes to the ground. He wrote "unqualified" on my folder, turned on his heel, and left. I was overcome by a wave of relief, which for the first time revealed to me how great my terror had been, and by the sense of shame which remains with me to this day.[40]

In private conversation twelve years later, Fallows told me that, given the chance to do it again, he would have refused induction and gone to prison.

I think I believe him.

THE RESTORATION OF IDEALS

But it seems so inadequate to leave it at that: with a reaffirmation of the cliche that, in the end we all have to live with ourselves. Perhaps it might be more appropriate to conclude, not with an invocation, but with a story.

On September 9, 1965, a Navy pilot named James B. Stockdale was shot down on a routine bombing mission over North Vietnam. He was to spend the next seven and a half years in prison, and to win the Congressional Medal of Honor for his resistance and leadership of the other prisoners. On the day of his shootdown, then-Commander (now Vice Admiral, retired) Stockdale was the archetypal fast-track naval officer: Annapolis graduate, fighter pilot, former test pilot, advanced degrees at Navy expense, all the right assignments, a sure bet for flag rank.

Stockdale was also something more. While doing postgraduate work at Stanford University, he'd discovered philosophy. He'd read the classics, particularly Aristotle and the Stoics, with interest, but with mixed emotions. He considered himself, and was, the consummate technological man, equally adept at managing machinery and men. What, he wondered, made these counsels of patience in adversity, and of the necessity of personal honor, so compelling to a man unaccustomed to non-manageable situations?

The answer was provided in the prison system of North Vietnam.

For the North Vietnamese, American prisoners represented a major potential asset. By inducing them to make public statements condemning the war, they could have enormous propaganda value; they could enable the North Vietnamese, as one interrogator put it, "to win this war on the streets of New York."[41] Techniques for persuading the prisoners to cooperate included torture, irons, solitary confinement, and an absolute prohibition upon communication between prisoners.

What Stockdale, and nearly all the other prisoners, discovered, was that the traditional sources of ethical guidance were insufficient to maintain personal integrity over long periods of time. Military discipline, the Code of Conduct, patriotism, religious faith, all had their uses. But in order to survive without disgrace, the prisoners had to create their own civilization, complete with special legal codes prescribing such items as how much torture to endure before making certain kinds of submissions, intellectual and cultural life (lectures on philosophy and engineering, for example, given by tapping in code on cell walls), and an absolute insistence on unity. Submission under torture brought no penalties in the civilization of the prisoners; failure to confess precisely what that submission had entailed, and failure to make the North Vietnamese start all over again the next day, did.[42] Never to grant yesterday's tortured concession free of charge today; never to endanger the others by pretending not to have submitted; always to value the common life of what Stockdale once referred to as an autonomous colony of Americans who happened to be located in a Hanoi prison—these became the civic virtues of the prison civilization. Once, tortured beyond endurance, Stockdale was told to write out the names of the leaders of the "central committee of the resistance." He wrote down the names of nearly every American he knew to be in prison. His interrogator threw the paper back at him, angrily shouting, "That's everybody!" Stockdale replied, "That's right. That's the central committee."[43]

Civic virtue in its purest form: concern for the common life, unwillingness to compromise that life, and mutual forgiveness in the face of inevitable personal shortcomings. And if there are to be any moral lessons drawn from the Vietnam experience, perhaps those are as good as any with which to start.

Three
POLICY

Present Danger, Present Choice

Whenever peace—conceived as the absence of war—has been the primary objective of a power or a group of powers, the international system has been at the mercy of the most ruthless member of the international community.

Henry A. Kissinger
A World Restored

A generation ago, the United States adopted containment as the essence of its global purpose. The result of this decision is now a matter of historical record: some initial (and enduring) successes in Europe and Korea, followed by promiscuous globalization, crisis after crisis, then disaster in Vietnam. Writing in 1968, Robert Tucker could blame it all on America's penchant for strewing alliances and guarantees across the planet. "What has happened," he concluded, "is that one of our promissory notes has had to be met."[1] The calling-in of that one small note very nearly bankrupted us.

What has happened since that note came due is now also a matter of historical record: a decade of American global passivity, Marxist successes around the world, and the relentless arms buildup of a Soviet Union which, contrary to containment's most basic postulate, has not mended its ways. Add to these facts the existence of a growing disarmament movement both in America and in Europe, an ever-more rickety Atlantic alliance, the volatility of the Middle East and Persian Gulf regions, and the judgment to be rendered on the future of containment seems clear.

It is failing. It has failed. Never intended as a permanent fixture of international life, its cost (both human and material) has become exorbitant, its successes ever more marginal, its ability to restrain Soviet and Soviet-backed expansionism questionable at best. A generation ago, the Soviet Union may have been hostile, but it was also comparatively weak. Today it is both hostile and strong, and with scant reason to believe that its adventures will be met with continued strong response.

But if containment no longer avails, what can take its place? What, short of the alternatives offered by World War III or neo-isolationism, can replace a doctrine aptly described by Aaron Wildavsky as "indispensable yet unsatisfactory?"[2] Or is, perhaps, the proper question: Should anything take its place? Must the United States continue to oppose Marxist expansionism at such horrendous costs, and at such horrendous risk? Our commitments and alliances do not contribute to our physical security. They jeopardize that security. Further, they entangle us in the affairs, not only of kindred societies, but of tawdry petty despotisms and third-rate incompetencies best disposed of by their own long-suffering peoples. Directly or indirectly, over half the American defense budget goes for protecting Europe; much of the rest purchases dubious security for peoples who may or may not desire our protection.[3] Why do it? Why subject both ourselves and the planet to the awful nuclear perils our resistance to Marxism must inevitably entail?

Many have argued that the risks and costs outweigh any possible benefits to the United States, that there is, for example, no gain in protecting trading partners whose protection threatens to bankrupt us. Many have called for a policy of "strategic disengagement"—not neo-isolationism *per se*, but realistic acceptance of an uncontrollable world (a world made more perilous by our attempts to control it), renunciation of containment, and prudent readjustment to new economic realities. As Earl Ravenal, an ardent and articulate advocate of disengagement, has written:

> . . . if we are to achieve disengagement, we must make our policy deliberately neutral toward a wide range of differential strategic conditions and outcomes in the world. We will be able to afford this orientation only if we hedge and insulate. But even these are not enough. To sustain a strict and consistent disengagement, our decision-making system must adjust its most fundamental presumptions—about the relevance of threats, the calculus of risks, and the nature of the national interest.[4]

Ravenal defines this "readjustment" with chilling succinctness:

> Because I propose . . . more restrained and national
> strategies, that does not mean that I take "the threat" as
> trivial or nonexistent. . . .
>
> On the contrary, the essence of the non-interventionist
> position is that it takes threats very seriously. But it accepts
> some foreign "losses" for fundamental reasons that have to
> do with preserving the integrity of our political and social
> system. Non-interventionists have not been blind to the fact
> that neutrality to the differential outcomes of foreign situa-
> tions might itself have an effect on those situations, and not
> always a pleasant one. *They foresee the losses, but they
> weigh and discount them.*[5] (Italics added)

In other words, why not just withdraw, hope for the best,
self-insure whenever possible, and make such accommoda-
tions as may be necessary in a world where only one superpower, the Soviet Union, exercises its ability to intimidate, intervene, and invade?

Before answering this question, it is necessary to ask another: Were the United States to withdraw from the world,
what might the Soviets do? And why?

THE PRESENT DANGER

The analysis of any foreign threat revolves around two issues: capabilities and intentions. A capability does not automatically equate to an intention of using that capability, although it may beget such intentions. Conversely, intentions
without capabilities may be meaningless, or they may impel
the creation of the necessary capabilities. As I write, the capabilities and (present) intentions of the Soviet Union *vis-à-vis* the
United States and its interests seem to be these.

The Soviet Union (and only the Soviet Union) possesses the
ability to destroy the United States by nuclear attack. While
there is no reason to believe that the Soviet Union intends to

do so, neither is there any evidence that the Soviet Union will ever consent to the surrender, or even the substantial diminution, of this capability. Nor is there any reason to believe that the United States (Reagan's Strategic Defense Initiative notwithstanding) will ever be able to protect itself from such destruction.

The Soviet Union (and only the Soviet Union) possesses the capability of severing America's sea and air lines of communication with the world (including much of the Western Hemisphere). There is no reason to believe that, in event of war or crisis, the Soviet Union would not use its naval and air forces, and the global base structure which sustains them, to mount what could well be a virtual blockade of America—a blockade which the United States might not be able to break, short of escalation to nuclear weapons.

The Soviet Union (and only the Soviet Union) possesses the capability to invade Western Europe. While there is no overwhelming evidence that the Soviet Union intends such an invasion (and good reason to believe that it does not), neither is there any evidence that the Soviet Union will ever surrender this capability.

The Soviet Union (and only the Soviet Union) possesses the capability of invading and conquering the oil lands of the Persian Gulf. There is no reason to believe that this capability will decrease, and increasing reason to believe that it might someday be used.

The Soviet Union (and only the Soviet Union) possesses, through its allies, clients, and surrogates, the capability of manipulating and co-opting revolutionary movements throughout the world. There is no reason to believe that Soviet intentions are other than the steady increase of this type of activity.

Finally, the Soviet Union still claims for its ideology a universal relevance which justifies unlimited violence across the planet.

Of course, Soviet intentions are affected by numerous factors: countervailing power, internal Soviet requirements and confusions, personal rivalries among leaders, transient opportunism, etc. Kennan recognized this fully, and the factors he enumerated a generation ago still hold. But the Soviet Union of the 1980s is a far different entity from the USSR of the late 1940s. It has indeed evolved, albeit in a way neither Kennan nor anyone else might have predicted a generation ago. Any new American strategy must, at the outset, take notice of this fact.

"Decadent but deadly"—so Dimitri Simes has characterized the present Soviet Union.[6] A stagnant society, a failed ideology, a system trapped by both its history and its rigidities, the present USSR has brought forth perhaps the most sterile civilization ever known. And, perhaps, it may not be averse to using its military forces in order to mitigate the effects of its own economic incompetence and spiritual malaise. At least, the contours of such a possibility are clear. They have been suggested in a recent book which may well do for this generation what Kennan's writing did for the last.

In a masterful short exegesis, *The Grand Strategy of the Soviet Union*, Edward N. Luttwak has offered a theory of Soviet motivation and conduct every bit as compelling as Kennan's.[7] In Luttwak's schema, the Soviet Union has evolved through five more-or-less distinct phases. In the beginning, Lenin's Bolsheviks offered the world the first successful Communist revolution, and various ethnic groups within the old Russian empire a new possibility: a transnational confederation based, not upon ethnic Russian dominance, but upon Marxist ideals. In the beginning, the promise seemed at least plausible, and not unattractive; indeed, many non-Russians (such as Stalin) held high positions in the young Bolshevik state. Non-Russian adherents were eagerly sought and advanced.

Both the global and ethnic promises failed, the former more rapidly than the latter. In the aftermath of World War I, the possibility of world communist revolution sparked by the Russian example became increasingly chimerical. The Soviet Union entered into its second phase, that of "socialism in one country" via the enslavement and expenditure of an entire generation. Ethnic Russians, by far the most educated and technically adept group within the pre-World War II USSR, began to assume an increasing share of power as industrialization proceeded. The German invasion of 1941, Luttwak's third phase, put an end both to Stalin's industrialization experiment and to any possibility of non-Russian minorities wielding real power. Unable to arouse the Russian people to anti-Nazi resistance on the basis of Marxist ideology, Stalin prudently reverted to a program of Russian ethnic chauvinism. By 1945, what had originally been envisioned as a multi-ethnic confederation had become a new Russian empire in which ethnic Russians, a minority, held almost complete power.

But the truly kairotic period of Soviet evolution proved to be the fourth. Between 1945 and the mid-1970s, Russian dominance solidified, while persecution of non-Russian minorities increased. Simultaneously, however, it became apparent that:

— The promise of communism in Russia would not and could not be fulfilled. The state had not and would not wither away. Far from it: The state and party had evolved into a massive, self-perpetuating bureaucracy, devoted primarily to the maintenance of its own institutional power and prerogatives. The vanguard of the proletariat had become a parasite on Soviet society as a whole, creating and exacerbating the very problems it allegedly existed to solve. Communism in the USSR had become, in effect, a protection racket.

— The promise of economic abundance would not and

could not be fulfilled. Russia, a country which before World War I had been one of the world's great grain exporters, could no longer even feed herself, thanks almost entirely to the inherent shortcomings of social-ized agriculture. Further, the industrial sectors had proven themselves systemically unable to produce con-sumer goods in necessary quantities and desirable qual-ities for the domestic market, and were utterly unable to compete in world markets. Save for raw materials and weapons, the Soviet Union simply had—and has —nothing to offer the world, and had become—and is —dependent upon the non-Marxist world for food, technology, and an increasing array of consumer goods.

— The ideology was bankrupt. Further, alternative creeds, such as Christianity, resurgent Islamic funda-mentalism, and ethnic consciousness (not to mention simple desire for freedom) were claiming more and more adherents. In an empire barely fifty percent eth-nic Russian, such divisiveness could only prove inflam-matory.

— Most of all, as the structural and spiritual failings of Marxism-Leninism-Stalinism became institutionalized, the military power at the disposal of the Kremlin had undergone a quantum expansion, an expansion all the more significant, given America's post-Vietnam self-disarmament. To be sure, Russia had always been mili-tarily powerful, but its might had been primarily defen-sive in nature; its conquests usually came as re-conquests, achieved after the homeland had been in-vaded, the invader over-extended, and then expelled (all at horrendous cost). Beginning in the 1960s, how-ever, the nature of Soviet military power changed drastically. A fully mechanized army, a new blue water, three-ocean navy, a greatly enhanced aviation capabil-ity, and a new naval infantry (a kind of Marine Corps) made the Soviet military an offensive instrument in

> every sense of the word. In short, beginning in the
> 1960s, the Soviet military began to evolve from a
> large, rather clumsy, primarily defense and satellite-
> occupation force, into an establishment designed to
> fight almost anywhere but within the Soviet empire.

Thus, according to Luttwak, the Soviet Union changed over
half a century from revolutionary, messianic experiment to
moribund empire, the last of the great European land empires. Now, the fifth stage has been reached, in which old-
fashioned imperial aggrandizement, as opposed to ideological
expansion, may serve to justify the regime's existence and as-
suage its inadequacies. Luttwak posits a basic dilemma faced
by the ruling oligarchy of an empire which finds itself both
"poorer and more powerful" than it could ever have imagined
possible:

> . . . the long-term pessimism of the Kremlin leadership is
> not assumed as fact, but merely put forward as theory.
> Quite separately, it is argued that—also for the first time—
> Soviet leaders old and new have *operational confidence* in
> their armed forces, specifically that they now have good
> reason to believe that the Soviet armed forces can conduct
> offensive operations with speed and precision, to win clean
> victories in short order against a variety of potential ene-
> mies in a variety of settings—so long as the risk of a nu-
> clear reaction by the victim is low, and the Soviet forces
> themselves do not need to employ nuclear weapons to ac-
> complish their goals.[8]

In sum, concludes Luttwak, the Soviet leadership, possessed of both a sterile empire subject to numerous internal
stresses, and a military instrument of global reach and offensive design, may find the temptation to use that instrument
overwhelming.

But toward what ends? Here Luttwak argues that the
USSR, a classic land empire, has fallen prey to the classic mal-

ady of land empires: the need to keep expanding in order to protect what one already has. The logic of empire is simple enough. Buffer zones gradually become integral parts of the empire, requiring new buffer zones, etc. Rome built walls in Britain in order to protect Italy. In the present instance, Luttwak suggests, the most logical Russian targets would be China and Iran. Neither country has a long history of unification; Russia could easily dismember both, taking northern Iran and western China, while permitting the existence of truncated countries unable to mount a successful reconquest.

Beyond this, Luttwak also suggests (as have a number of other writers) that Soviet power might be used to blackmail Europe into what is commonly, if erroneously, known as "Finlandization." Under this arrangement, Western Europe would gradually be reduced to an economic appanage of the Soviet empire, trading with the Russians on increasingly unfavorable terms, subsidizing that empire's economic incompetence, in exchange for not being invaded. The arrangement might never be made explicit, or even called by its proper name of slavery. But it certainly does seem more logical for the Soviet Union to view western Europe (and Japan) more as a source of tribute than a possible conquest.

In sum, if Luttwak is correct, a new Soviet grand strategy may be emerging, one quite different from Kennan's original formulation, and potentially far more dangerous. Where Kennan argued for a certain Soviet caution, and posited a willingness to back off when confronted by force or show-of-force, the new strategy implies a signal lack of reticence, short of the nuclear threshold. It is a strategy based, not upon ideology or xenophobia, but upon simple extortion. Nuclear extortion might do the job; conventional extortion alone might suffice. The loss of Communist China as a *de facto* Western ally would no doubt exacerbate the potential for extortion, as would a more imminent Soviet threat to Persian Gulf oil. Also, where Kennan claimed that Russian communism must inevitably "mellow," due to its inherent contradictions and inefficiencies, Luttwak's scheme suggests that the opposite is more likely, especially if initial attempts at extortion prove successful. Further, it must be pointed out that recurrent Soviet attempts at economic reform must inevitably fail. Not only is the system inherently non-reformable, due to its own illogical over-centralization, but real reform would endanger every segment of society. As Michael Ledeen has pointed out, reform has absolutely no constituency: not among the elites who would lose their *raison d'être*, not among the masses of functionaries and workers who would have to acquire new skills (and maybe actually do an honest day's work), and not among the large criminal minority.[9]

And, final irony, the American defense buildup, especially the Strategic Defense Initiative, may well push the Russians into early use of their conventional capability for extortion purposes. Not because they fear the rapid erosion of their power, but because they simply can't afford to keep up the competition.[10]

This, then, is the present danger: an essentially sterile empire, beset by both systemic economic inadequacies and rising ethnic unrest, with nothing to offer the world save a promise not to destroy it, compelled—*perhaps*—to imperial expansion as an alternative, to genuine internal reform. Throughout history, such imperial expansions have been common, as have those instances when nations unable to resolve their domestic dilemmas turn to foreign adventures as a palliative. And while history never quite repeats, there is no reason to suppose that such actions, such aggressions, are impossible, or even unlikely, today.

THE PRESENT CHOICE

Could the United States survive in a Soviet-dominated world? Yes, it could. Could the United States survive as a *de facto* Soviet tributary state? Yes, it could. The United States could, tomorrow, disengage from the world, keep a minimal nuclear deterrent on hand to discourage that kind of black-mail, dismantle its armies, trade with a Marxist world on whatever terms the Marxists might care to provide and, as Earl Ravenal once put it, "live less well, but live."

Or shall it be the American purpose on this planet to offer the world alternatives to either nuclear catastrophe or a slowly descending Marxist New Dark Age? Shall it be the purpose of the United States, not to contain armed Marxism anywhere and everywhere, and not to work toward some millennial day of Russian "mellowing," but to save whatever can be saved of the global structure of freedom?

If the answer is, *no*, then all questions of military claim and obligation, of defense budgets and force structures, and indeed of honor, became irrelevant. If the answer is, *yes*, then the relevant question becomes, *how*?

Engagement and Reform

The Soviet Union is the only country in the world surrounded by hostile communist powers.

Jeffrey Record
Revising U.S. Military Strategy

As I write, the United States possesses no clear declaratory global strategy. We have, instead, a potpourri of commitments, doctrines, interests, psuedo-interests, and a mélange of competing bureaucratic preferences. We have no shortage of cliches. But we have no clear sense of what we wish to accomplish in this, the post-containment age.

Further, as I write, the United States possesses a military establishment beset by multiple, and potentially fatal, structural shortcomings. To say this is not to deny that the Reagan rearmament program has wrought substantial improvements in conventional capability; indeed, it would be hard to throw a trillion dollars at anything and not come away with some improvements. Nor is this to deny that the quality of military personnel has improved dramatically over the past few years. It has, and the United States currently fields what is arguably the finest peacetime military in its history. But it is also a military with problems that no expenditure, and no amount of personal dedication, can cure.

The United States, I am suggesting, possess neither a coherent grand strategy nor the military wherewithal to execute such a strategy, should one ever come to exist. Until the time as such a strategy does exist, a strategy which could (and indeed must) enjoy the support of the American people, and until such time as the American military is tailored to the demands of that strategy, it would be worse than futile even to consider asking the American people to sanction renewed conscription. For, even though the major military deficiency lies in manpower, conscription alone can't solve that problem. Drafting a million or two million men (and women) into a military that can't use them properly accomplishes nothing. But conscription in support of a coherent grand strategy, a strategy supported by a properly structured military establishment, constitutes sufficient grounds to justify reinstating the conscriptive military claim.

Fortunately, both the rudiments of a new grand strategy and the first signs of a rejuvenating military now exist. The strategy has been variously described as "minimal containment," "selective engagement," and "strong-point defense."[1] I prefer a simpler term, engagement, as a clear alternative to disengagement, and also a clear distinction from containment. Engagement recognizes both the limits of American power and the futility of global perimeter defense, but nonetheless undertakes to counter the Soviet threat, using an array of instruments, some military, others not. Engagement readily concedes that some losses, even major losses, will be inevitable. Engagement holds, however, that some such losses may, from the Western point of view, even be desirable. Like a martial arts expert who uses his opponent's strength against him, engagement seeks not simply to defeat Soviet expansionism, but to accept (and perhaps encourage) it in areas where it must prove exceptionally costly and ultimately self-defeating.

However, if engagement is to succeed, it requires a completely restructured military. Happily, many of the necessary reforms are well underway: changes in doctrine, training, weaponry, administration, and (*mirabile dictu*) procurement. Some of these are the product of an unusual tandem of "military reformers"—a loose-knit group of civilian analysts, Congressional types and rising officers who have no desire to repeat their Vietnam experiences. Unfortunately, though, the most imporant issue has not yet been addressed. *Have we created a military that is too large for small contingencies, too small for large ones, and structured around the fact that conscription is currently politically impossible?*

To answer this question, it is necessary first to define the strategy of engagement and then consider the problem of military structure and reform.

ENGAGEMENT

The strategy of engagement is based upon two premises. First, it assumes that, while the Soviet Union certainly can't be considered the source of all the world's evils, it is nonetheless America's only significant adversary. Therefore, it is important that the course of events (of global structure of freedom) wherever possible, weaken that adversary. Forty years ago, Kennan argued correctly that only those areas which greatly enhance Soviet economic strength need be actively defended. Whatever form of government the non-Marxist world manages (or mismanages) its affairs under, should not be a great American concern. What matters is to prevent major accretions of Soviet power, whether by conquest or extortion.

Second, engagement requires that, whenever possible, efforts be made to exacerbate the economic, ethnic, and religious tensions within the Soviet empire. Obviously, these efforts must be primarily non-military, and not directed toward the destruction of the empire. But they do have two military aspects. Occasionally, it may be more useful to surrender territory in order to exacerbate those tensions. And it may also prove useful to support various indigenous resistance movements, not to the point of American intervention, but as a constant irritant around the empire's borders. Historically, such irritants, when continued long enough, have severely damaged otherwise seemingly impregnable imperial structures.

Operationally, engagement requires clear geographical selectivity, and the structuring of forces in accordance with the following priorities:

1) The defense of Western Europe, including the prevention of "Finlandization" as well as of outright conquest. It is often noted that the war least likely to occur, a massive Soviet invasion of Central Europe, would also be the most di-

sastrous for the United States. Therefore, American forces in Europe must remain coupled to the nuclear deterrent. But should they also be adequate to absorb a Soviet conventional thrust and (in conjunction with allies, of course) to stabilize the front? Is such adequacy even possible? The answer to this question is probably yes. But if a serious conventional defense of Europe is to be undertaken, then conscription will have to be reintroduced. Otherwise, American forces, no matter what their quality, must remain mere nuclear "trip-wires." At the moment, American policy on European defense has been to spend money on a force much too large to play the "trip-wire" role, and much too small to mount a successful defense.

2) Defense of the Japan/South Korea complex, again to prevent "Finlandization" as well as conquest. Again, conventional forces should remain coupled to the nuclear deterrent. And again, the question arises: Are the forces committed to Asian defense too large for small contingencies and too small for large ones?

3) Defense of the Southwest Asia/Persian Gulf oil lands and adjacent sea lanes, but only until the Western need for the area diminishes to some tolerable level. After that, the region may be deemed superfluous, and the West might well look with indifference upon the incorporation of more Islamic nationalities in the Soviet empire. However, the defense of the area for the next two decades or so poses special problems. Acquisition of the Persian Gulf oil fields doesn't enhance Soviet economic strength the way unimpeded access to NATO Europe or Korea/Japan would, but even successful Western defense of the fields could leave them virtually destroyed. Thus, if the United States is to act as "executive agent" for the West and Japan/Ko-

rea (neither NATO nor Asian allies can operate effectively here), a special type of force will be required: one which may not entail renewed conscription, but which must certainly be both expensive and large.

4) Prevention of a situation in Central America that would precipitate an uncontrollable exodus of refugees to the United States. The problem of the "feet people" is already acute. The United States has effectively lost control of its southern border and cannot regain it, short of militarizing that border: an act which would generate politically distasteful consequences. Further, are the American people really prepared to start machine gunning refugees at the Rio Grande? I rather think not. But if the problem is severe, and can only be worsened by Marxist victories in Latin America, this does not necessarily mandate the overt use of American force in the region. Indeed, the use of force would probably be disastrously counter-productive. Rather, the United States should adopt a policy of "counter-co-optation."

Historically, Soviet-backed regimes throughout the lesser-developed world have come to power via a two-stage process. First, Marxists join with (or dominate) genuinely popular movements against domestic or colonial despotisms, sundry tyrannies all too often supported by the United States. Then, after revolutionary success, there follows the gradual elimination of the non-Marxist revolutionaries and the establishment of totalitarianism. This repression and establishment normally takes several years.

But what if this two-stage process could be extended to three: revolution to rid a country of its dictatorship or colonial regime, followed by the standard Marxist bid for total control, followed by the armed refusal of those who did not throw off one set of tyrants in order to submit to another, far worse? And what if such refusals could avail themselves of those tactics and methods which have proven so successful in disrupting governments across the planet? And what if such armed refusals could enjoy American support?

For several years, an experiment of this nature has been underway in Nicaragua. To date, results have been decidedly mixed. Two things, however, seem clear. First, the American people do not particularly relish the prospect of supporting guerrillas, a fact not lost upon a number of grandstanding Congressional types. This popular distaste has several sources: so-called Vietnam syndrome, reluctance to aid and abet the more unsavory aspects of insurgency, dislike of the secrecy with which such support must normally be given. But American support for insurgencies has strong historical roots (What *was* the *Maine* doing in Havana Harbor, anyway?) and it is not at all clear that aid given insurgent movements (as opposed to governments) generates any inevitable momentum toward American intervention. If anything, aid given to such movements should generate far less impetus toward the use of American force than aid given to recognized states.

Second, it is clear that the Reagan administration, despite its rhetoric, has no firm policy for supporting insurgent and resistance movements, in Nicaragua, Cambodia, Afghanistan, or anywhere else. Engagement requires such support: low-cost, low-risk aid to freedom fighters that can possibly prevent further Marxist victories (or merely drain Marxist resources) on a global basis. There is, no doubt, something unattractive about a superpower—a democratic superpower, at any rate—engaging in this kind of activity, especially in conflicts where the issues grow complex and the contending parties alike in their tactics. But it may prove necessary.

5) Finally, engagement holds that, with the exception of support for insurgencies and resistance movements, most of the Third World may be written off as either indefensible or not worth the price of defense.

The strategy of engagement, in sum, involves a firm strongpoint defense of Europe and Japan/Korea, a firm (if not eternal) defense of Southwest Asia and the Persian Gulf, and an increasing reliance on indigeneous para-military forces either to prevent Marxist domination or to render that domination damnably expensive. Other, non-military elements are also involved; dealing with trade, technology transfers, disinformation, etc. On the military level, engagement mandates the prudent, last-resort use of American conventional forces only in areas of vital interest. But can the United States structure and man the necessary forces? The answer is unclear.

REFORM

Several years ago, in the aftermath of the Iranian rescue debacle, a new phrase entered the lexicon: "military reform movement." Since then, this phenomenon has attracted a steadily increasing visibility, and an intermittently increasing influence. Given the facts of an American military which (Grenada notwithstanding) has not won a single significant victory since 1950, and a Pentagon seemingly intent upon maximizing financial waste, the emergence of such a movement would appear both beneficial and long overdue. And so it would be, were it not for the fact that no such "movement" exists.

In reality, the military reform movement has been less a force than a *tendance*, a surprisingly inchoate congeries of participants, interests, and predilections. Reformers include several dozen Congressmen, Senators, and legislative assistants, loosely organized around a staffless Congressional Military Reform Caucus which has yet to enact a single significant piece of legislation. The "movement" also includes perhaps a hundred civilian analysts and consultants, a few media publicists, and some (usually anonymous) active-duty officers who prefer to study the reformers rather than be linked to them. Much of the movement's literature is highly technical and available only in specialized publications. Some of the vital ideas have never been committed to paper at all.

Nor do the concerns of the reformers coincide. Some worry about force structures and weapons; others ponder tactics and doctrine; still others criticize military education and the "managerial mindset"; an increasing number focus on the assorted horrors of procurement and administration; a few concentrate on reform of the Joint Chiefs of Staff.[2] Most of the reformers advance their pet ideas with an almost messianic fervor; aptly, Richard Betts has condemned much of the movement for unwarranted faith in the curative powers of single solutions.[3]

To be sure, many, indeed most, of these proposals have considerable merit. Some are currently being adopted, or at least tested, by the military. But, in the end, the movement, whatever its beneficial effects, has failed even to pose, let alone answer, the fundamental question:

Reform for what geostrategic purpose?

It is all well and good to document the inadequacies of particular weapons (an easy enough task), or to attack wasteful procurement and accounting practices (nowadays a daily occurrence), or outdated tactics, or whatever. But in the absence of a comprehensive and coherent sense of what these forces are to be used for, most reform measures are destined to remain palliatives, at best. After all, does it matter how well the ship or tank or whatever works, or how much it costs, if the question, *what do we need this for?* has not been (or cannot be) satisfactorily answered.

Happily, however, a debate concerning overall American grand strategy has gotten underway. Some of the participants are military reformers; most would not consider themselves such. This grand strategic debate, which transcends the specifics of reform, provides a highly useful means of approaching the question of whether or not conscription is needed. The contours of the debate are complex, the nuances many. In essence, this debate addresses the issue of converting purpose into capability: Shall the conventional power of the United States reside primarily in its land forces, or in its naval and air capabilities? This is the question which must be answered before determining what to buy, or whether or not to draft.

The debate, however, is far from new. It is, in a sense, as old as the Republic itself. Until the present era, the answer has been relatively clear.

For most of its history, the United States has chosen to let the bulk of its power reside in its naval and (since World War II) air forces, raising large armies only after the commencement of hostilities, disbanding them almost immediately thereafter. For most of its history, this policy made eminent sense. Since the Mexican War, the United States has faced no significant continental adversary; nobody is currently about to invade. Further, for most of its history, the United States eschewed "entangling alliances" which might have required large peacetime ground forces. Further still, until after the Second World War, the United States could count on numerically superior allies who would provide the bulk of the manpower, and do most of the dying, in any conflict. Finally, the United States could count on months and years of mobilization and training time after hostilities commenced. Thus, for most of its history, large standing armies were both philosophically repugnant and militarily unnecessary. The United States was free to concentrate on doing what it did best: applying economic power and technology to war, and that at a relatively leisurely rate.

Unfortunately, this happy condition no longer obtains. The numerically greatest of America's former allies, Russia, is now the foe. America's present allies are no longer expected to absorb the first blows alone. In Europe, Americans will be dying as fast as Germans or Dutch. In areas such as the Persian Gulf, where the indigenous manpower supply is minimal and where NATO can't function effectively, Americans will do nearly all the fighting. Finally, given the magnitude of Soviet forces available for short-to-no-notice attacks, it is uncertain whether any war would last long enough for American economic and industrial superiority to have any effect . . . *or for renewed conscription to make any difference*. Although predictions are always suspect, it seems reasonably clear that any major Soviet-American conflict, i.e., *any* Soviet-American conflict would either be settled or go nuclear rather quickly.

All of which is to say that America's future wars, unlike those of the past (except Korea), are likely to be "come-as-you-are," fought with the men and materiel immediately available.

How shall American forces be structured to cope with this fact? How, also shall American forces be structured to deal with the unexpected: with minor, and perhaps lengthy, conflicts against enemies other than the Soviet Union? Shall American forces be, as in the past, primarily naval and air forces, or shall some new accommodation be made to the exigencies of ground combat with the Russians? And if so, how?

Over the last few years, two seemingly polar answers have emerged. One is more-or-less traditional, the "maritime/power projection strategy." The other is a somewhat updated version of the "Continental/coalition" strategy in vogue since 1949, but never seriously implemented. Both strategies start from the assumption—the axiom, really—that there currently exists a dangerous mismatch between American obligations and resources, especially in the event of simultaneous high and low intensity conflicts. Both strategies concede that, in their pristine forms, neither can meet all of America's defense needs. Both concede that their arguments can be used in justification for expenditures which may or may not be vital. Also, both argue that, unless their alternative is given primacy, the United States faces potential disaster.

The "maritime/power projection" strategy has been argued most forcefully by defense analyst and military reformer Jeffrey Record. He concerns himself with two items, one military, the other political. Europe, in this analysis, has become an unremunerative drain on American defense capabilities, due both to the absolute costs of credible conventional defense and the seeming irresolution of our allies. Given increasing demands for American forces elsewhere, the United States can no longer afford to do what Europeans should be doing for themselves:

> The time has come for the United States to begin withdrawing most of its ground forces from Europe, and to adopt a global strategy based on sea power and the ability to project power from sea to shore.
>
> Such a revolution [a post-1945 revolution] in America's strategic outlook and military posture is dictated by two seminal events: the steady and apparently irreversible disintegration of the North Atlantic Treaty Organization as an instrument capable of mustering an adequate forward defense of Western Europe, and the emergence of a host of new threats to vital U.S. security interests in Southwest Asia . . .[4]

In Record's formulation, the United States must revert to a more-or-less unilateralist strategy, concentrating on non-NATO contingencies. If Europe chooses not to defend itself, i.e., to run the risks of either invasion or "Finlandization" after American withdrawal, so be it: The United States should not squander its resources. Rather, the United States should bring home (and then demobilize) its Europe-based ground forces, leaving only tactical air forces as a "trip-wire" guaranteeing early American involvement (but not heavy casualties) in any future conflict. Concurrently, the United States should begin emphasizing rapidly deployable naval and amphibious forces capable of Persian Gulf operations, creating an extremely expensive power projection capability which, ironically, would be used to defend oil of far more importance to Europe than to the United States.

Is Record's prescription as radical as its sounds? Not really: All he is demanding is for Europe, a population-superior and wealthy aggregate, to provide its own ground forces while the United States reverts to doing what it has always done best. He calls it "a new transatlantic division of military labor."[5] Further, he assumes that, faced with an American *fait accompli*, Europe would indeed begin to provide more of its own defense. In either case, however, Record sees no future for American ground forces in Europe: a conclusion shared by a number of far-from-dovish legislators, such as Senator Sam Nunn, who periodically introduces legislation calling for at least a token American withdrawal.

Is Record correct? In part, no doubt. But to the extent that he is, he contradicts his own basic premise: the ongoing disintegration of NATO as a viable instrument. Despite its perpetual failure to meet its own military spending goals—a failure now extending over three decades—NATO has remained a remarkably stable alliance. A congeries of sixteen vastly different nations, each beset by significant disarmament movements, NATO has nonetheless managed to survive institutionally since 1949: no small accomplishment. Further, unlike the United States, nearly all NATO countries (Great Britain being the major exception) have retained peacetime conscription, and most have generated significant reserve forces. Further, it is far from clear that NATO Europe lacks the "will" to defend itself. No one can predict such things prior to the crisis, but the democracies of Western Europe have, historically, been willing to defend themselves when defense became imperative. Europe may have been pacifist on August 31, 1939. A week later, the situation was quite the opposite.

At the other conceptual extreme lies the "continental/coalition" theory, perhaps argued most forcefully by former Ambassador and Pentagon official Robert Komer. Komer, while conceding a certain (inevitable) disarray and (equally inevitable) parsimony among America's European allies, argues that, come what may, NATO must remain the central concern of American strategy. Indeed, he concludes that our allies, despite their occasionally annoying qualities, provide a great deal:

> Indeed, *the single greatest remaining U.S. strategic advantage over the U.S.S.R. is that we are blessed with many rich allies, while the Soviets have only a handful of poor ones.* . . . They also fear their own forced allies, while we fear for ours.[6] (Italics Komer's)

For Komer, as for Record, the loss of Europe would be a political, economic, and (not least of all) cultural and spiritual disaster. Unlike Record, however, Komer argues that Europe's defense must remain the primary American purpose. This defense requires land power; no amount of American naval and air power, no matter how useful, could defeat the Soviet Union on the plains of Central Europe. Nor would it do much good to retain control of the Atlantic sea lanes if the reason for control—access to Europe—is lost. Indeed, if Europe went under, how long could America even retain such control? Thus, Komer contends, American strategy must be based upon a renewed emphasis on ground forces within a strong coalition framework, not upon an increased American unilateral ability to conduct peripheral operations. NATO, in his formulation, must become more of what it was originally intended to be: a truly integrated multinational force, not a collection of more-or-less unco-ordinated entities. It can be done, he suggests, if it is done patiently, discreetly, and with keen sensitivity to the nuances of domestic European politics. And while the United States might also, indeed must also, act as "executive agent" for NATO in the Persian Gulf, since it alone possesses the requisite amphibious capabilities, even this should be done as part of a co-ordinated effort.

But can Europe be defended conventionally: Can a Soviet assault be, if not repelled, then at least contained without use of nuclear weapons? Here, again, it is impossible to offer an indisputable prediction. A raw count of numbers might not seem that encouraging. A crude comparison of NATO and Warsaw Pact forces indicates the following:

CATEGORY	NATO	WARSAW PACT
Divisions	93	176
Tanks	14,460	42,600
Anti-Tank	15,300	32,200
Artillery	11,500	35,000
Combat Vehicles	35,700	75,000
Attack Helicopters	775	960
Fighter-Bomber/Attack	1,975	2,250
Interceptor	780	4,195[7]

However, in military affairs, as in business, raw data tell only part of the story. Omitted here are qualitative differences in equipment, reliability of troops, size differentials (Soviet divisions tend to be smaller than NATO, and certainly American counterparts), operational competence, etc. The picture would seem to be far less glum, were the following conditions to obtain:

— Ample warning time prior to attack. Invasions require preparations; the power that Russia could *effectively* utilize in a European invasion varies directly with the thoroughness of preparations—most of which would be visible to the West.[8]

— Early and effective Western mobilization

— The political situation in Eastern Europe

— The possible role(s) of the People's Republic of China in diverting forces otherwise intended for European use.

But even assuming long warning times, prompt response, turmoil in the satellites, and a co-operative China, could the Warsaw Pact (or at least its Soviet component) actually be defeated on the ground? The answer would appear to be, perhaps. Western weaponry and doctrine continue. Further, Western Europe is no longer open territory, ideal for massed tank attacks. It is a kind of megalopolis, with large urban concentrations interspersed with numerous small villages, forests, etc. Attacking mechanized forces, such as the Soviet Army, could be canalized and impeded. Some analysts, such as Steven Canby, have suggested that NATO abandon its doctrine of defense at the inter-German border and substitute the following strategy:

— Creation of an inter-German border barrier zone, designed to impede (but not stop) a Soviet mechanized advance.

— Use of reserves to defend individual pockets such as villages and forests, while main-force units are withheld for an eventual counter-attack.[9]

Would such a strategy be politically acceptable in peacetime? At the very least, it would mean the *de facto* acceptance of permanent German division and commitment to a policy which would sacrifice large numbers of mobilized reservists in the first few days while conserving the active-duty forces. It would also require that the current American plan for European defense, known as "Deep Strike," work almost perfectly. Under the "Deep Strike" concept, the attacking Soviet forces would be permitted entry, while succeeding echelons and resupply capabilities would be attacked on the *eastern* side of the inter-German border. All in all, it would seem a rather risky affair.[10]

In sum, then, the current grand strategic debate revolves around two poles, both of which concede the central importance of NATO Europe, and then diverge radically on the question of how to protect it. Whether NATO can remain a viable alliance is a matter of dispute, as is the question of whether Western Europe can be defended conventionally. Neither concept, the "maritime/power projection" or the "continental/coalition" enjoys a monopoly of truth. And, interestingly, both sides hold the same opinion of the Reagan defense program.

They consider it a disaster.

Both Record and Komer recognize that conventional rearmament, after the depredations of Vietnam and the neglect of the 1970s, was long overdue. Both, however, fault the Reagan administration for its seeming lack of any coherent strategy beyond procurement. For Komer, the current naval buildup, with its 600 ship goal, leads to "maritime strategy by default."[11] Record, on the other hand, condemns the administration's strategic promiscuity, i.e., the policy that the United States must be prepared to fight in several theatres simultaneously, and may indeed *choose* to initiate hostilities in non-NATO theatres after a European war begins. According to this doctrine of "horizontal escalation," the United States might, for example, choose to respond to a Soviet invasion of Western Europe by attacking Cuba, or Hungary, or whatever, or by using American aircraft carriers to sink the Soviet navy in port (I've yet to meet a single sailor willing to undertake *that* trip.). To Record, as to Komer, "horizontal escalation" seems ludicrous, at best.[12] And both men conclude that, despite the trillion dollars spent over the last few years, American strategy is going nowhere, except back to the old, disastrous notion of globalized containment.

Indeed it has. Perhaps the greatest irony of the current defense program is that, despite its cost, it has failed to remedy any of the fundamental flaws in American conventional planning. It has substituted money for thought; it has, in the final sense, been irrelevant to America's real conventional needs. In order to demonstrate this, it is necessary to consider the problem of force structure in a bit of detail.

A military force is not an abstraction. Nor does it spring into existence *ex nihilo*. It is designed to accomplish specific types of tasks. In the broadest sense, only two kinds of Western conventional force exist. A territorial defense force does precisely that: It defends territory. It operates in or around its national boundaries in order to deter or defeat such threats as may approach. A territorial defense force tends to be heavily armed, logistically complex, designed for high-intensity warfare, and very large. It usually draws its manpower via conscription, and depends upon a large pre-trained and quickly mobilizable reserve. Such policies are politically acceptable because a territorial defense force usually exists to fulfill an unambiguous, even sacrosanct mission: defense of the homeland. Israel, Switzerland, France, and the Federal Republic of Germany provide examples of such forces.

Alternatively, a force may be expeditionary in nature, i.e., designed to fight well away from home. An expeditionary force tends to be lightly armed, logistically austere, small, and dependent upon costly air and sea transport and control assets. Unlike territorial defense forces, expeditionary forces may not know ahead of time who or where they will fight; the Falklands War provides a perfect example of this uncertainty. Further, expeditionary forces are usually structured for low-intensity (albeit often protracted) duty in conflicts whose prosecution may or may not enjoy overwhelming public support. For these reasons, expeditionary forces are best manned by volunteers, and, as a rule, should not be dependent upon reserve mobilization.

By the grace of God and geopolitics, the United States does not fight on its own soil. Its forces are therefore, by definition, expeditionary. But for a generation now, the United States has maintained a *de facto* territorial defense force in Europe: a small (currently about four divisions) forward deployment presumably reinforceable by units rushed from the continental United States in an emergency. Also for a generation now, the United States has tailored most of its CONUS (Continental United States)-based divisions for the special requirements of European war: heavy mechanization, large formations, massive logistics. By preparing most of its Army for European war, the United States has, in effect, created a second territorial defense force *on the wrong continent*. At one time, American naval and air supremacy, Soviet lethargy, and a firm political consensus on America's NATO commitment made this policy at least defensible. No more: And palliative measures such as prepositioning divisional equipment in Europe, then flying over the troops cannot substitute for formations deployed and ready overseas.

The problem, however, goes beyond this. By tailoring its divisions for European combat, the Army has historically circumscribed its capabilities in other areas. In order to evade this fact (a fact glaringly apparent when the first Army divisions reached Vietnam), defense planning has, for a generation, been based upon a fallacy. Ground forces have been decreed "general purpose," i.e., available for duty anywhere. This is nonsense.[13] Ships and aircraft may be considered, within broad limits, as globally employable. Ground forces rarely are. Differences of possible terrain, climate, mission, and enemy all demand that ground forces specialize: some for jungles, some for deserts, some for Europe, etc. But for a generation, American defense planning has presumed that forces structured for NATO contingencies could fight anywhere (assuming, of course, that they could even be transported to the battlefield in the first place). And, for the past few years, planning has proceeded according to a second fallacy: that such forces (again, assuming the existence of adequate lift) could be moved from CONUS to almost anywhere on short-to-no-notice.

Happily, this situation is beginning to change, due at least in part to the efforts of military reformers. Wisely, the Army has chosen to specialize, to create, in effect, different forces for different contingencies: heavy divisions for Europe, light, rapidly deployable divisions for use in the Persian Gulf and elsewhere.

As I write, the Army fields sixteen active divisions (two more are planned for early activation).[14] Of these eighteen divisions, ten have been slotted for NATO use. Four reside in Europe. Six more, based in the United States, would be flown to Europe in an emergency, draw prepositioned equipment from storage, and be on line within ten days of alert (the so-called "10/10 Plan"). Up to five divisions are currently allotted to the Central Command (the old Rapid Deployment Joint

Task Force) for use in the Persian Gulf. These divisions would be light infantry, rapidly deployable and small. The Army has already begun the conversion of two formerly heavy units; both of these divisions now being light infantry. One additional division resides in Korea. One has been designated an experimental formation. Two divisions are paratroop and air assault specialty units, and not prudently committed to sustained ground combat. On the surface, the arithmetic seems clear:

NATO (10/10) ----------------- 10 Divisions*

Central Command ------------ 5 Divisions**

Korea --------------------------------- 1 Division

Experimental --------------------- 1 Division

Airborn/Assault ---------------- 2 Divisions

19 Divisions

However, three problems present themselves. The first, and perhaps least serious, is that only a small fraction of the necessary sea and air lift assets exist. Even assuming that an enemy remains sufficiently sporting not to attack American ships and aircraft enroute to the battlefield, only a small part of American CONUS-based divisions can even be moved. A second, and more serious problem, is that the arithmetic does not reflect real needs. By some estimates, as many as 23 divisions would be needed to cope with a Soviet invasion of Europe, while five divisions in the Persian Gulf might not im-

---

*May include Airborne/Air Assault divisions
**May include Marine Divisions (three are currently active).

press, let alone defeat the two dozen or so coming down from the Soviet Union. But the third, and by far the most fundamental problem is this:

The people necessary to man even the present force structure do not exist. Nor do the people necessary to translate Reagan's purchases into military power. Nor are they likely to, so long as the United States clings to a potentially disastrous doctrine known as the Total Force Policy.

THE TOTAL FORCE POLICY

As I write, the Reagan defense buildup seems to have taken on its final form.[15] Its major conventional components are these:

— An eighteen division active Army, structured for both NATO and non-NATO contingencies.

— A three division/three air wing Marine Corps.

— A 600-ship navy, based upon a projected fifteen aircraft carrier battle groups, three battleship (surface action) groups, plus sea control, amphibious, fast sealift, and submarine assets.

— An Air Force based around 79 fighter/attack squadrons, plus air transport assets.

— Ongoing improvements in sustainability and readiness.

To man this force, the United States currently operates with about 2,150,000 men and women.[16] This would be adequate, indeed perhaps excessive, were it not for one fact:

That the United States must be prepared to fight almost anywhere on short-to-no-notice. That is, the United States must prepare its *expeditionary* forces with minimal reliance upon reserve mobilization. But for a decade, American policy has been exactly the opposite, and the Reagan administration has consistently refused to face the fact that active-duty manning levels are utterly inadequate for the kinds of wars America may be called upon to fight. The Reagan administration has, instead, chosen to rely on a doctrine first formalized by Nixon as a means of justifying the end of conscription: the Total Force Policy, which decrees that part-time reservists constitute *the full equivalent of full-time active-duty personnel for purposes of planning and employment, and are available for short-to-no-notice mobilization and commitment anywhere.*

No policy could be more erroneous.

The full extent of American dependence on part-time reservists is not well-known. However, the part-time reserves currently account for about one-half of America's combat capability, and two-thirds of America's combat support capability. At least nine of the active Army divisions require massive reserve "roundout"—the addition of whole battalions and brigades in order to reach combat strength. Nearly half of the Air Force's tactical aircraft reside in the reserves. Further, the Individual Ready Reserve (servicemen and women released from active duty but with residual military obligations) is, by some estimates, not only about 300,000 individual replacements short, but also unable to contact half the people in its computer banks, due to outdated phone numbers and addresses.[17]

To be sure, reserve forces are a vital component of any large military establishment. They possess three inherent advantages.

First, they are comparatively cheap (cheap, of course, being a function of what one wishes to purchase). Although the initial costs of procuring comparable regular and reserve (or National Guard) units are the same, reserves do save money in the long run. Lower operating tempos, equipment usage rates, salaries, retirement costs—all combine to render reserve units between 30% and 70% cheaper than their regular counterparts. Flying squadrons tend to be near the low end of this savings range, ground combat units near the top.

Second, reserves provide a convenient means of augmenting scarce military skills (doctors, technicians, etc.) or for providing skills not needed in peacetime (graves registration, civil affairs, etc.) Further, certain types of units have consistently shown themselves combat ready. Reserve and Air National Guard flying squadrons, for example, routinely outperform their active counterparts, a happy condition due largely to the fact that reserve pilots tend to be more experienced.

Third, reserves can easily be mobilized to man the "CONUS rotation base"—the U.S. system of bases and training facilities—in the event of emergency, thus freeing their active counterparts to fight.

Balanced against these three advantages—cheapness, skill acquisition, and CONUS support—are six disadvantages which make reserves utterly inappropriate for large-scale use in expeditionary forces.

First, training time is limited. It is simply not reasonable to expect reserves (again, with notable exceptions) to maintain the skills and proficiencies necessary for successful short-to-no-notice deployment.

Second, reserve equipment is traditionally inferior to that of the active forces: marginal to obsolete "hand-me-downs." Reserve equipment is inadequate in both quantity and quality for rapid mobilization, and simply equipping reserves with up-to-date gear upon mobilization allows no training time.

Beyond time and equipment limitations, however, lie four problems peculiar to short-to-no-notice mobilization. To borrow a cliche from the 1960s, "What if they gave a war and nobody came?" Pentagon planning routinely assumes that about 70% of reservists summoned would show up on time, ready to go. A series of mobilization exercises conducted over the past decade, however, have pointed to much lower results, and one need not question either the patriotism or the courage of the weekend warrior to understand why. Both practical considerations and the inevitable political problems mobilization generates would suggest the need for more realistic planning.

Fourth, assuming that large numbers of reserves could be assembled in hours or days, there is no guarantee that adequate transportation would be available.

Fifth, assigning reserve units as units perpetuates one of the great advantages of reserves: unit cohesion. Historically, however, reserve units have been broken up and used as gap fillers. Placing strangers together mere days before combat results not in unit cohesion, but in groups of strangers running around the battlefield.

Sixth, what would be the political costs of serious reserve mobilization . . . and of mass casualties in some hometowns, none in others? This issue has gone largely unaddressed. Historically, however, reserve mobilization has been politically possible only *in extremis*, and only for uses which enjoy overwhelming public support.

None of this is meant to criticize the reserves themselves. The Total Force Policy has contributed to the creation of what is without doubt the finest reserve establishment in American history. But to repeat:

No nation which plans on fighting well outside its own borders, on short-to-no-notice, should depend upon reservists for the bulk of its forces. This is what the United States has been doing for over a decade and, if present trends continue, the dependence will only worsen. The Reagan administration has chosen to evade the issue, preferring to concentrate upon acquisition. But the time is fast approaching when it will be necessary to ask, "Can the United States continue to play this kind of game with its military forces, its future security, and perhaps the fate of the world?"

Conscription

While the Constitution protects against invasion of individual rights, it is not a suicide pact.

U.S. Supreme Court
U.S. v Mendoza-Martinez (1963)

Late in 1982, the Military Manpower Task Force, a high-level committee appointed to study the All-Volunteer Force (AVF) reported to President Reagan. The AVF was, the task force concluded, in fine shape. Almost *en passant*, the Task Force Report noted that it "did not question the programmed military strengths of the active and reserve components, or the mix between active and reserve forces."[1] This might be compared to the Food and Drug Administration certifying a medicine without inquiring into either what diseases it was intended to treat, the proper dosages, or possible side effects. To be sure, the Task Force report accurately depicted an AVF both good and getting better. But it evaded the critical question: Are there—can there be—enough of them? The Task Force's mandate, no doubt, forbade that type of questioning: forbade it, no doubt, because the answer would have raised an issue the Reagan administration has consistently refused to face: the need for renewed peacetime conscription.

For the past ten years, the issue of conscription has occupied a position on the continuum of American political concerns somewhere between saving the whales and reviving the Confederacy. No one has been drafted in over a decade. No emergency requiring mass mobilization appears imminent, or even probable. Conscription has utterly no domestic constituency; no politician wins votes by advocating it. Even the military, rightly fearful of reviving civilian antagonisms, has urged conscription only intermittently—an advocacy usually followed, especially since 1981, by angry rebuttals from the civilian masters of the Pentagon. And, without doubt, the AVF has succeeded . . . at least when measured by those statistical indices aptly labelled pseudo-criteria by many soldiers.[2] Can it fight? Hopefully, we'll never know.

The AVF may be superb, as far as it goes. The problem is, it doesn't go far enough. Even without a new war, military manpower requirements must inevitably rise. All those new ships must be sailed, those planes flown and maintained, those new (albeit smaller) divisions fleshed out. The reserves may also be superb, but they can't reasonably be expected to spend Tuesday in Boston and the following Sunday in the Persian Gulf. Yes, the statistics are good, the quotas (for the most part) being met. But the statistics of quality do not address the issue of quantity, and the quotas reflect the bureaucratically expedient and the economically possible, not the hard realities of possible war.

What can be done?

There are, in essence, only three possibilities, if a force structure adequate to meet America's obligations is to be achieved. The first is the radical relaxation of entry standards, coupled with further increases in the use of women. There is nothing inherently wrong with this, except that it would result in a less qualified, less deployable force. A second alternative has been proposed by Professor Charles Moskos, a "two-track" volunteer force with low pay (but high GI benefits) for one-term volunteers.[3] The third alternative is to reintroduce some form of peacetime conscription, a practice abhorrent to many and capable of arousing the most violent reactions among those affected.

Conscription is not simply a means of obtaining military manpower. It is, as Eliot Cohen has well noted in *Citizens and Soldiers*, also a political institution which reflects the deepest values of a society.[4] Further, suggests Cohen, the United States, almost alone among major powers, has failed to achieve a satisfactory long-term system of recruitment. He attributes this failure to conflicts of basic value (the love for freedom versus the sense that sacrifice should be spread evenly), the politically controversial nature of possible wars, and not a little military poor judgment. Thus, to suggest that conscription must be reinstated for purely military reasons is to ignore the larger values which may have given birth to those reasons.

And it is to ignore the fact that in a sense, conscription—our attitudes toward it and practice of it—tell us not only what we're willing to defend, but also what we are.

THE CONTOURS OF DEBATE

Modern public discourse has an unusual trait. The whole often adds up to less than the sum of its parts. Perhaps nowhere is this phenomenon of reverse synergy more evident than in the contours of the post-Vietnam draft versus voluntarism debate.

How often it seems that the parties to the dispute fail even to agree on what it is they dispute. "My concern," said Richard Hunter at a Hoover Institution conference on the draft, "is not for the U.S. military. My concern is for the U.S. society."[5] An interesting approach to a military question, and well-countered at the same conference by Lewis Gann's observation that: "The object of creating an army is not to be fair, it is not to be economical. It is to fight a war. . . . Which kind of army, a volunteer army or a conscript army, is likely to do the job better?"[6] A reasonable question, albeit one which leaves out the myriad social and political issues involved. Or perhaps not so reasonable a question, given manpower expert Martin Binkin's rejoinder that "we really don't know how to measure whether a conscription army can fight better than a volunteer army [short of actual combat]."[7] Now add to this the array of admissions and collected insights of the sociologists, economists, lawyers, libertarians, and pacifists, the accumulated tonnage of government, government-financed, and privately-funded studies, surveys,and prognostications, and it's really no wonder that any public discussion rapidly devolves into a chaos of competing rationales and partial verities. Then add to this the current lack of national consensus over whether or not an imminent danger exists, the sense of security provided by a trillion dollars of defense spending, and the present administration's refusal to discuss manpower problems at all, and it's hardly strange that chaos inevitably ensues.

This is unfortunate. It is also unnecessary. For the conscription versus voluntarism debate to have any meaning, it must proceed on the basis of a minimal commonality of meaning. That minimal commonality, I would suggest, is this.

First, there must be at least a perceivable justification for conscription. In the present instance, I have suggested, that need flows from the serious mismatch between America's military commitments and the manpower needed to fulfill them on short notice.

Second, if conscription is ever to be justified, it must be seen as an activity—like military service itself—as unique, set apart, and subject to its own standards. If conscription (and military service) are simply one form of human activity, to be measured by the same standards which apply to others, then conscription is inherently unacceptable, except in the most dire emergency. In point of fact, all objections to conscription (save for the time-honored "Don't feel like it") are based upon this type of reductionism.

There are, in essence, only three kinds of reductionist argument against conscription. The first, which might be termed the libertarian, holds that conscription is a form of involuntary servitude, and therefore prohibited by the Constitution. "[I]t should be noted," writes Doug Bandow, "that the whole draft debate is really quite curious. In no other occupation, service, or profession are people conscripted; nowhere else do people seriously suggest replacing voluntarism with conscription. The military is dangerous, of course, but that does not make it unique."[8] According to this reasoning, the purpose of the military is to protect the polity, not to violate its most basic principles. Concludes Bandow: "The principles on which this nation was founded must be defended in a manner consistent with the principles themselves."[9]

The problem with this reasoning is that it overlooks two facts. The first, and more obvious, is that for any principles to exist at all, the society which adheres to them must also exist. No other occupation or profession provides the *sine qua non* of a polity's existence. An exception from the voluntaristic ethic characteristic of liberal society has always been made. Sometimes it has taken the form of compulsory militia duty, other times of equal (male) liability to a selective or random draft.

The second fact which this argument overlooks is that a person must *consent* to be drafted. Other options, including prison or voluntary exile, are available. As Aristotle well understood, free will and compulsion can co-exist. And as Mack Owens has noted, not without a certain irony: "Men can be 'coerced' by laws of their own making."[10]

A second argument against conscription holds that it is inherently inequitable, and therefore unacceptable. This might be termed the economic argument; expressed in its simplest form, it contends that conscription constitutes a "tax in kind." President Nixon's Commission on an All-Volunteer Armed Force, which successfully urged an end to the draft, used this reasoning, as has economist Milton Friedman.[11] Beyond simple economics, this argument holds that the mere fact that some serve while others do not renders conscription unacceptable, notwithstanding the fact that all (at least all males) may have been equally liable to the draft, as in the lottery system.

The argument is correct; conscription short of universal service (a practical and economic impossibility, a military waste) is indeed inequitable. So is what happens to people after they enter the military. Some become computer experts, others drive trucks. Some fight, some don't. Some live, some die. But the vital question here is not individual equity; it is—

or should be—common survival. Or, to ask it another way: Which comes first, surival or equity?

To be sure, any form of conscription should be as equitable as possible. No doubt the greatest failure of Vietnam era conscription (until 1970) was its *de facto* exemption of the middle class. But equity cannot be the overriding concern, for it leads to either of two extremes: no conscription at all, or else the waste of universal service. Since not all are needed in the military, or can serve, this has often led to proposals for universal national service with both military and civilian options. The idea has been around for at least a century. In its most recent incarnation, Senator Gary Hart has called for a presidential commission to investigate the possibility anew. Writing in the *New York Times*, Senator Hart suggested that such a program would not only solve the military's upcoming (if not present) problems, but also provide for vital civilian programs in places such as Appalachia and Harlem. Senator Hart concluded:

> Universal national service is an opportunity for this generation to achieve with its hands what others sought to buy with their dollars. We can do more for our young people by asking more from them.[12]

This is utterly pernicious, not only in its desire to insure equity by spreading hardship, but also for its attempt to use conscription for social engineering. If the military claim is to have any validity, it must remain unique, not one part of a package of involuntary servitudes. Many worthwhile projects could no doubt be performed in such a manner; they should not, however, be performed as an enforced alternative to defense.

The final argument holds that conscription is unnecessary because the day of mass armies is over, that any war would go nuclear long before conscription made any difference. Perhaps. But the point of renewed conscription would be to have an army in being which could keep a war from going nuclear, not to create an army after the outbreak of hostilities.

In sum, then, three arguments against renewed conscription: the libertarian, the economic, the nuclear. Each is flawed. But then, so are most of the arguments offered in favor of conscription.

Conscription is not justifiable on the grounds that military service is every citizen's moral obligation. It is not. The moral obligation of defense resides in the state—in its constitutional mandate to provide for the common defense. Individual moral obligation begins when the individual consents to serve, and whether that consent be obtained by voluntarism or conscription matters not at all.

Nor is conscription ever justified by the alleged benefits of military service to the individual. A person may indeed "grow up" in the military, or learn a skill, or return a patriot, or whatever. But these are ancillary benefits, and no more justify conscription than they do military service itself.

Nor is conscription justifiable because it represents the most efficient means of procuring manpower, itself a highly debatable proposition. The military exists for the society, not vice versa.

Nor is conscription justifiable because it was done in the past. The current situation is unique in both its complexity and its dangers, many of which can be dealt with by means other than the draft—indeed, by means other than military.

Conscription is only necessary if it is to be the American purpose to offer this planet alternatives to either Armageddon or a communistic New Dark Age. Nothing else, nothing less, can justify its return. And if it is not to be the American purpose to provide such alternatives, then much of the currently standing military should be dismantled immediately, and the wealth and talent contained therein turned to the problem of American welfare in the world that would ensue.

Conclusion

A long twilight struggle . . .

John F. Kennedy
Inaugural Address

Can it be the American purpose to offer such alternatives? Perhaps.

Should it be? I think so, yes.

Would this purpose, when given form as military policy, require resumption of the draft? Most probably, although a future draft need not resemble any of the past. I have no specific proposals to offer, save for the obvious suggestion that it should be as equitable and bearable as possible. And perhaps it should contain a feature found only rarely in the history of American conscription, although commonly in the history of the militia: what Eliot Cohen has called the idea of intermediate obligation.

The United States, alone among Western powers, presumes that its forces, volunteer or conscripted, can be used anywhere, for any purpose. No other country makes such assumption, certainly not for its draftees. In some countries, such as Israel and Switzerland, soldiers may assume that they will not be used far beyond their homelands for wars of uncertain justification. Other countries, such as France, the Netherlands, and West Germany, legally enjoin themselves from sending their draftees beyond their borders unwillingly.

Perhaps some sort of intermediate obligation could be included in a future American draft: some kind of guarantee that no conscript would be sent involuntarily outside the United States, except upon declaration of war, or Congressional resolution. Those services not relying on draftees—the Navy, Air Force, and Marines—would be exempt from this proviso, as would certain designated units within the Army. Politically, such a policy might do what the War Powers Act has tried (probably in violation of the Constitution) to do: find a workable twentieth century balance between the powers of the Commander in Chief, the prerogatives of the Congress, and the legitimate post-Vietnam caution of the people. (Further, it would offer the individual draftee at least a minimal assurance that his services would not be used in ventures of dubious morality or unclear purpose.) Militarily, such a policy would be cumbersome. But it may be better than no draft at all.

Will any of this come to pass? Will President Reagan, now a man with no more elections to face, begin to address this issue? Will the politicians? Will the military? Will the media? In short, will there be the kind of full, intense, and open debate which must come to pass before the American people give their consent to renewed conscription? At the moment, it is difficult to tell.

But this much, at least, seems clear.

If it is to be the American purpose to offer this planet alternatives to slavery and holocaust —to practice a prudent civic virtue on a planetary scale—it will require the full participation of the American people, as well as their tacit consent. And if it does become our purpose, and we succeed, we will have become what the Founding Fathers always sensed we might become.

The last, best hope of man.

Notes

CHAPTER ONE
FOUNDATIONS OF THE CLAIM

[1]James Turner Johnson, *Can Modern War Be Just?* (New Haven: Yale University Press, 1984), pp. 29, 11.

[2]Ibid.

[3]See Roland H. Bainton, *Christian Attitudes toward War and Peace* (New York: Abingdon Press, 1960).

[4]See Henry Paolucci, ed., *The Political Writings of Saint Augustine* (South Bend: Regnery-Gateway, 1962), pp. 162–183.

[5]William V. O'Brien, *The Conduct of Just and Limited War* (New York: Praeger, 1981), p. 3.

[6]John Courtney Murray, S.J., *Morality and Modern Warfare* (Council on Religion and International Affairs, 1959), p. 14. See also Kenneth W. Thompson, ed., *Moral Dimensions of American Foreign Policy* (New Brunswick: Transaction Books, 1984).

[7]See Leon Friedman, ed., *The Law of War: A Documentary History*, 2 vols. (New York: Random House, 1972). See also Gerhard von Glahn, *Law among Nations: An Introduction to Public International Law*, 4th ed. (New York: Collier-Mac-Millan, 1981). See also Michael Howard, ed., *Restraints in War: Studies in the Limitation of Armed Conflict* (Oxford: Oxford University Press, 1979).

[8]Quoted in Hannah Arendt, *On Revolution* (New York: Penguin Books, 1965), p. 13.

[9]Cicero, *De Officiis* (Cambridge: Harvard University Press, 1968), p. 37.

[10]See Paolucci, ed., *Political Writings of Saint Augustine*, pp. 162–183.

[11]Thomas Aquinas, *Summa Theologica II*, No. 15, Q. 40 (art. 1). The historical development of the *jus ad bellum* has been the subject of a rich and growing literature. See O'Brien, Bainton, and Johnson, works cited above. See also two additional volumes by James Turner Johnson, *Ideology, Reason and the Limitation of War: Religious and Secular Concepts 1200–1700* (Princeton: Princeton University Press, 1975) and *Just War Tradition and the Restraint of War: A Moral and Historical Inquiry* (Princeton: Princeton University Press, 1981). See also two volumes by Paul Ramsey, *War and the Christian Conscience: How Shall Modern War Be Conducted Justly?* (Durham: Duke University Press, 1961) and *The Just War: Force and Political Responsibility* (New York: Scribner's, 1968). See also Michael Walzer, *Just and Unjust Wars: A Moral Argument with Historical Illustrations* (New York: Basic Books, 1977).

[12]Robert F. Drinan, S.J., *Vietnam and Armageddon: Peace, War, and the Christian Conscience* (New York: Sheed and Ward, 1970), p. 13.

[13]James W. Douglass, *The Non-Violent Cross: A Theology of Revolution and Peace* (New York: Macmillan, 1968), p. 176.

[14]Paul Ramsey, *War and the Christian Conscience*, p. 198.

[15]Ramsey, *The Just War*, p. 56.

[16]For an opposing view by a just war advocate, see James Turner Johnson, *Can Modern War Be Just?*

[17]See Richard A. Falk, ed., *The International Law of Civil War* (Baltimore: Johns Hopkins University Press, 1971). See also Michael Howard, ed., *Restraints in War* and Geoffrey Best, *Humanity in Warfare* (New York: Columbia University Press, 1980).

[18]Michael Walzer, *Just and Unjust Wars*, p. 108.

[19]See G. A. A. D. Draper, "Wars of National Liberation and War Criminality," in Howard, ed., *Restraints in War*, pp. 139–162. See also William Safire, "Rights for Terrorists?" *New York Times*, November 15, 1984. p. A–31.

[20]U.S. Department of Defense News Release #609–84, "Remarks Prepared for Delivery by the Honorable Caspar W. Weinberger: 'The Uses of Military Power,'" November 28, 1984.

CHAPTER TWO
RESPONSES TO THE CLAIM

[1]See Michael Walzer, *Just and Unjust Wars: A Moral Argument with Historical Illustrations* (New York: Basic Books, 1977), pp. 251–268.

²Michael Harrington, "Politics, Morality and Selective Dissent," in James Finn, ed., *A Conflict of Loyalties: The Case for Selective Conscientious Objection (New York: Pegasus, 1968), p. 227.*

³*American Heritage Dictionary of the English Language* (Boston: Houghton Mifflin, 1969).

⁴Michael Walzer, *Obligations: Essays on Disobedience, War, and Citizenship* (Cambridge: Harvard University Press, 1970), pp. 5, 22.

⁵See Roland H. Bainton, *Christian Attitudes toward War and Peace* (New York: Abingdon Press, 1960).

⁶"Resolution of the Continental Congress, July 18, 1775," reprinted in John O'Sullivan and Alan Meckler, eds., *The Draft and Its Enemies: A Documentary History* (Urbana: University of Illinois Press, 1974), pp. 12–13.

⁷U.S. Supreme Court, *U.S. v Macintosh*, 283 U.S. 605 (1931) at 623.

⁸U.S. Congress, "1940 Selective Training and Service Act," reprinted in O'Sullivan and Meckler, eds., *The Draft and Its Enemies*, p. 181.

⁹U.S. Supreme Court, *U.S. v Seeger*, 380 U.S. 161 (1965) at 166–168.

¹⁰Ibid at 163.

¹¹Ibid.

[12]U.S. Supreme Court, *Welsh v United States*, 398 U.S. 333 (1969) at 333.

[13]Ibid at 334, 341, 336.

[14]Ibid at 341, 338.

[15]Ibid at 334, 341.

[16]Tim O'Brien, *If I Die in a Combat Zone* (New York: Laurel, 1969), pp. 30–31.

[17]John Locke, "Second Treatise of Government," in *Two Treatises of Government* (New York: Mentor, 1968), p. 392.

[18]Harry Jaffa, "Military Service: The Nature of the Obligation," *Washington Times*, November 5, 1982, p. 10.

[19]Paul Ramsey, *The Just War: Force and Political Responsibility* (New York: Scribner's, 1968), p. 92.

[20]Robert Tucker, *The Just War: A Study in Contemporary American Doctrine* (Baltimore: Johns Hopkins University Press, 1960), p. 148.

[21]U.S. Supreme Court, *Gillette v United States*, 401 U.S. 437 (1970) at 437.

[22]Andy Mager, "I Won't Register for the Draft," *New York Times*, January 5, 1985, p. 21.

[23]Thomas Hobbes, *De Cive* (Garden City: Doubleday, 1962), p. 87.

[24]Thomas Hobbes, *Leviathan* (New York: Dutton, 1940), p. 87.

[25]Ibid, p. 115.

[26]Ibid.

CHAPTER THREE
THE AMERICAN REVOLUTION

[1]Lois Schwoerer, *"No Standing Armies!" The Anti-Army Ideology of the Seventeenth Century* (Baltimore: Johns Hopkins University Press, 1974), p. 188.

[2]J. G. A. Pocock, ed., *The Political Works of James Harrington* (Cambridge: Cambridge University Press, 1977), p. 131.

[3]Ibid, p. 443.

[4]See Schwoerer, *"No Standing Armies!"* and Pocock, *Political Works of James Harrington.* See also J. G. A. Pocock, "Civic Humanism and Its Role in Anglo-American Thought," in *Politics, Language, and Time: Essays on Political Thought and History* (New York: Atheneum, 1970), pp. 80–103 and "Machiavelli, Harrington, and English Political Ideologies in the Eighteenth Century," *William and Mary Quarterly* (October 1965), pp. 549–583. See also Lawrence Delbert Cress, "Radical Whiggery and the Role of the Military: Ideological Roots of the American Revolution," *Journal of the History of Ideas* (January 1979), pp. 43–60.

[5]See John Shy, "A New Look at the Colonial Militia," in _A People Numerous and Armed: Reflections on the Military Struggle for American Independence_ (New York: Oxford University Press, 1976), pp. 21–33. See also John Shy, "American Society and Its War for Independence," in Don Higginbotham, ed., _Reconsiderations on the Revolutionary War: Selected Essays_ (Westport: Greenwood Press, 1978), pp. 72–82. For general histories see Russell Weigley, _History of the United States Army_ (New York: Macmillan, 1967), pp. 3–28, and John K. Mahon, _History of the Militia and the National Guard_ (New York: Macmillan, 1983), pp. 2–44.

[6]Quoted in Cress, "Radical Whiggery," p. 57.

[7]See John Shy, "The Legacy of the American Revolutionary War," in _The Legacies of the American Revolution_ (Utah State University Press, 1978), pp. 45–46.

[8]John Shy, "The Military Conflict Considered as a Revolutionary War," in _A People Numerous and Armed_, pp. 45–46.

[9]John C. Fitzpatrick, ed., _The Writings of George Washington_, 39 vols. (Washington: U.S. Government Printing Office, various dates), vol. 6 (1932), pp. 4–5; vol. 7 (1932), p. 106, pp. 53–57.

[10]Ibid, vol. 6, pp. 110–112.

[11]John O' Sullivan and Alan Meckler, eds., _The Draft and Its Enemies: A Documentary History_ (Urbana: University of Illinois Press, 1974), p. 18.

[12]Fitzpatrick, ed., _Writings of Washington_, vol. 8 (1933), p. 78.

[13]Fitzpatrick, ed., *Writings of Washington*, vol. 20 (1937), pp. 114–115.

[14]Bernard Bailyn, *The Ideological Origins of the American Revolution* (Cambridge: Harvard University Press, 1967), p. 56.

[15]Ibid, p. 51.

[16]Gordon S. Wood, *The Creation of the American Republic* (Chapel Hill: University of North Carolina Press, 1969), p. 38.

[17]Pocock, "Civic Humanism," p. 97.

[18]See Lawrence Delbert Cress, *Citizens in Arms: The Army and the Militia in American Society to the War of 1812* (Chapel Hill: University of North Carolina Press, 1982). See also Cress, "Republican Liberty and National Security in American Military Policy as an Ideological Problem: 1783–1789," *William and Mary Quarterly* (January 1981), pp. 73–96.

[19]Cress, *Citizens in Arms*, pp. 108–109.

[20]Alexander Hamilton, "The Federalist #23," in Clinton Rossiter, ed., *The Federalist* (New York: Mentor, 1963), p. 153. For an opposing view see Leon Friedman, "Conscription and the Constitution: The Original Understanding," *Michigan Law Review* 67:8 (June 1969), pp. 1493–1552.

CHAPTER FOUR
VIETNAM

[1]Hannah Arendt, *On Revolution* (New York: Penguin, 1963), p. 56.

[2]Ibid, p. 57. Arendt's quote taken from Lord Acton, *Lectures on the French Revolution* (Noonday Paperback Edition, 1959).

[3]Norman Podhoretz, *Why We Were in Vietnam* (New York: Simon and Schuster, 1982), pp. 2–15. See also Fox Butterfield, "The New Vietnam Scholarship," *New York Times Magazine*, February 13, 1983, p. 26 and Peter Braestrup, ed., *Vietnam as History: Ten Years after the Paris Peace Accords* (Washington: University Press of America, 1984).

[4]John Lewis Gaddis, *Strategies of Containment: A Critical Reappraisal of Postwar American National Security Policy* (New York: Oxford University Press, 1982), p. 243.

[5]Quoted in Stephen E. Ambrose, *Rise to Globalism: American Foreign Policy 1938–1980*, 2nd ed. (New York: Penguin, 1982), p. 132.

[6]George F. Kennan, Doc. #861.00/2-246, in U.S. Department of State, *Foreign Relations of the United States 1946*, vol. 6, *Eastern Europe: The Soviet Union* (Washington: U.S. Government Printing Office, 1969), pp. 699–700.

[7]George F. Kennan, "The Sources of Soviet Conduct," reprinted in George F. Kennan, *American Diplomacy 1900–1950* (Chicago: University of Chicago Press, 1951), p. 113.

[8]NSC-68, reprinted in *U.S. Naval War College Review* 27:6 (May-June 1975), pp. 53, 54.

[9]See Adam Ulam, *The Rivals: America and Russia since World War II* (New York: Penguin, 1971).

[10]Kennan, "Sources," p. 120.

[11]Ibid, p. 120.

[12]NSC-68, p. 79.

[13]Kennan, "Sources," p. 128.

[14]NSC-68, p. 56.

[15]Gaddis, *Strategies of Containment*, p. 92.

[16]Lyndon B. Johnson, *The Vantage Point: Perspectives on the Presidency 1963–1969* (New York: Holt, Rinehart, and Winston, 1971), pp. 147–148.

[17]Doris Kearns, *Lyndon Johnson and the American Dream* (New York: Harper and Row, 1976), pp. 251–252. See also Robert J. Donovan, *Nemesis: Truman and Johnson in the Coils of War in Asia* (New York: Saint Martin's, 1984).

[18]See Daniel Ellsberg, "The Quagmire Myth and the Stalemate Machine," in *Papers on the War* (New York: Simon and Schuster, 1972), pp. 42–135. See also Larry Berman, *Planning a Tragedy: The Americanization of the War in Vietnam* (New York: Norton, 1982).

[19]Quoted in Donovan, *Nemesis*, p. 139.

[20]See Lawrence Freedman, *The Evolution of Nuclear Strategy* (New York: Saint Martin's, 1983), pp. 91–120.

[21]Quoted in Col. Harry G. Summers, "How We Lost," *The New Republic*, April 29, 1985, p. 22.

[22]Hendrik Hertzog, "Why the War Was Immoral," *The New Republic*, April 29, 1985.

[23]See Leslie Gelb and Richard Betts, *The Irony of Vietnam: The System Worked* (Washington: The Brookings Institution, 1979). For analyses by military officers see Col. Harry Summers, *On Strategy: A Critical Analysis of the Vietnam War* (Presidio: Presidio Press, 1982), and General Bruce Palmer, *The Twenty-Five Year War: America's Military Role in Vietnam* (Lexington: University Press of Kentucky, 1984). See also Guenter Lewy, *America in Vietnam* (New York: Oxford University Press, 1978).

[24]Paul M. Kattenberg, *The Vietnam Trauma in American Foreign Policy 1945–1975* (London: Transaction Books, 1980).

[25]Given in Nancy Zaroulis and Gerald Sullivan, *Who Spoke Up? American Protest against the War in Vietnam 1963–1975* (Garden City: Doubleday, 1984), p. 47.

[26]Ibid, pp. 157–181.

[27]Ibid, p. 127.

[28]Hannah Arendt, "Lying in Politics," in *Crises of the Republic* (New York: Harcourt, Brace, Jovanovich, 1972), p. 38.

[29]Lawrence M. Baskir and William A. Strauss, *Chance and Circumstance: The Draft, the War, and the Vietnam Generation* (New York: Knopf, 1978), p. 5.

[30]Thomas Power, *Vietnam: The War at Home* (Boston: G. H. Hall, 1984), p. 164.

[31]Zaroulis and Sullivan, *Who Spoke Up?* pp. 63, 258.

[32]See Peter Clecak, *America's Quest for the Ideal Self: Dissent and Fulfillment in the Sixties, and Seventies* (New York: Oxford University Press, 1983).

[33]Quoted in Kenneth Keniston, *Young Radicals: Notes on Committed Youth* (New York: Harcourt, Brace, Jovanovich, 1968), pp. 27, 26, 25.

[34]Quoted in Michael Useem, *Conscription, Protest, and Social Conflict: The Life and Death of a Draft Resistance Movement* (New York: Wiley, 1973), p. 237.

[35]Zaroulis and Sullivan, p. 82.

[36]Norman Mailer, *The Armies of the Night* (New York: Signet, 1968), p. 24.

[37]Ibid, p. 262.

[38]Ron Kovic, *Born on the Fourth of July* (New York: Pocket Books, 1976), p. 138.

[39]See Robert Jay Lifton, *Home from the War: Vietnam Veterans: Neither Victims nor Executioners* (New York: Simon and Schuster, 1973).

[40]James Fallows, "What Did You Do in the Class War, Daddy?" in A. D. Horne, ed., *The Wounded Generation: America after Vietnam* (Englewood Cliffs: Prentice-Hall, 1981), pp. 17–18.

[41]Jim and Sybil Stockdale, *In Love and War: The Story of a Family's Ordeal and Sacrifice during the Vietnam War* (New York: Harper and Row, 1984), p. 181. For other prisoner of war accounts see Senator Jeremiah A. Denton, *When Hell Was in Session* (Mobile: Traditional Press, 1982) and Lt. Col. John A. Dramesi, *Code of Honor* (New York: Norton, 1975).

[42]James B. Stockdale, *A Vietnam Experience: Ten Years of Reflection* (Stanford: Hoover Institution Press, 1984), pp. 142, 145.

[43]Stockdale and Stockdale, *In Love and War*, pp. 273–274 contains a fuller account.

CHAPTER FIVE
PRESENT DANGER, PRESENT CHOICE

[1]Robert W. Tucker, *Nation or Empire: The Debate over American Foreign Policy* (Baltimore: Johns Hopkins University Press, 1968), p. 10.

[2]Aaron Wildavsky, ed., *Beyond Containment: Alternative American Policies toward the Soviet Union (San Francisco: ICS Press, 1983), p. 3.*

[3]Richard Halloran, "Europe Called Main U.S. Arms Cost," *New York Times*, July 20, 1984, p. 2.

[4]Earl Ravenal, "The Case for Strategic Disengagement," in *Strategic Disengagement and World Peace: Toward a Non-Interventionist Foreign Policy*, Cato Papers #7 (San Francisco: Cato Institute, 1979), p. 21.

[5]Earl Ravenal, "Reagan's 1983 Defense Budget: An Analysis and an Alternative," *Cato Policy Analysis*, April 30, 1982, p. 14.

[6]Dimitri K. Simes, "The New Soviet Challenge," *Foreign Policy* 55 (Summer 1984), p. 113.

[7]Edward N. Luttwak, *The Grand Strategy of the Soviet Union* (New York: Saint Martin's, 1983). See also Wildavsky, ed., *Beyond Containment,* and Norman Podhoretz, *The Present Danger* (New York: Simon and Schuster, 1980).

[8]Luttwak, *Grand Strategy*, pp. 39–40.

[9]See Michael A. Ledeen, *Grave New World* (New York: Oxford University Press, 1985), pp. 149–198.

[10]Jerry F. Hough, "Could 'Star Wars' Foment a New Russian Revolution?" *Washington Post*, January 6, 1985, pp. C-1, C-4.

CHAPTER SIX
ENGAGEMENT AND REFORM

[1]See Aaron Wildavsky, ed., *Beyond Containment: Alternative American Policies toward the Soviet Union* (San Francisco: ICS Press, 1983). See also Robert W. Tucker, *The Purpose of American Power: An Essay on National Security* (New York: Praeger, 1981).

[2]Popular literature on military reform includes the following: Asa Clark, et al, eds., *The Defense Reform Debate: Issues and Analysis* (Baltimore: Johns Hopkins University Press, 1984), James Fallows, *National Defense* (New York: Random House, 1981), Edward N. Luttwak, *The Pentagon and The Art of War* (New York: Simon and Schuster, 1985).

[3]Richard K. Betts, "Dubious Reform: Strategism versus Managerialism," in Clark, ed., *Defense Reform Debate*, pp. 62–82.

[4]Jeffrey Record, *U.S. Strategy at the Crossroads* (Washington: IFPA, 1982), p. 1.

[5]See Jeffrey Record, *Revising U.S. Military Strategy: Tailoring Means to Ends* (McLean: Pergamon-Brassey's, 1984), chapter 6.

[6]Robert W. Komer, *Maritime Strategy or Coalition Defense?* (Cambridge: Abt Books with University Press of America, 1984), p. 27. For a good overview of the maritime versus coalition debate see Keith A. Dunn and William O. Staudenmeier, *Strategic Implications of the Continental-Maritime Debate*, CSIS Washington Papers #107 (New York: Praeger, 1984).

[7]U.S. Department of Defense, *Soviet Military Power 1984* (Washington: U.S. Government Printing Office, 1984), p. 74. For a more detailed, non-governmental assessment see International Institute for Strategic Studies, *The Military Balance 1984 (London: IISS, 1984).*

[8]See William P. Mako, *U.S. Ground Forces and the Defense of Central Europe* (Washington: The Brookings Institution, 1983).

[9]See Steven Canby, "Military Reform and the Art of War," in Clark, ed., *Defense Reform Debate*, pp. 126–146. See also F. W. von Mellenthin and R. H. S. Stolfi with E. Sobik, *NATO under Attack* (Durham: Duke University Press, 1984).

[10]Ibid.

[11]Komer, *Maritime Strategy*, p. 59.

[12]Jeffrey Record, "Jousting with Unreality: Reagan's Military Strategy," *International Security* 8:3 (Winter 1984), pp. 3–18.

[13]See William W. Kaufmann, *Planning Conventional Forces: 1950–1980* (Washington: The Brookings Institution, 1982).

[14]Charles Mohr, "To Modernize, the Army is Bringing Back Light Infantry," *New York Times*, November 25, 1984, p. E-3.

[15]Caspar W. Weinberger, *Annual Report to the Congress FY 1986* (Washington: U.S. Government Printing Office, 1985), p. 304.

[16]Ibid, p. 300.

[17]For a detailed analysis see Philip Gold, 'What the Reserves Can—and Can't—Do," *The Public Interest* 75 (Spring 1984), pp. 47–61.

CHAPTER SEVEN
CONSCRIPTION

[1]Military Manpower Task Force, *A Report to the President on the Status and Prospects of the All-Volunteer Force* (Washington: U.S. Government Printing Office, 1982), p. xiv.

[2]See Martin Binkin, *America's Volunteer Military: Progress and Prospects* (Washington: The Brookings Institution, 1984). For earlier assessments see General Andrew J. Goodpaster and Lloyd H. Elliott, eds., *Toward a Consensus on Military Service: Report of the Atlantic Council's Working Group on Military Service* (New York: Pergamon, 1982) and General Brent Scowcroft, ed., *Military Service in the United States* (Englewood Cliffs: Prentice-Hall, 1982).

[3]Charles C. Moskos, "Making the All-Volunteer Force Work: A National Service Approach," *Foreign Affairs* 60:1 (Fall 1981), pp. 17–34.

[4]Eliot Cohen, *Citizens and Soldiers: The Dilemmas of Military Service* (Ithaca: Cornell University Press, 1985).

[5]Martin Anderson, ed., *Registration and the Draft: Proceedings of the Hoover-Rochester Conference on the All-Volunteer Force*, Hoover Publication #242 (Stanford: Hoover Institution Press, 1982), p. 160.

[6]Ibid, p. 37.

[7]Ibid, pp. 33–34. For an excellent anthology on the draft and related issues see Martin Anderson, ed., *The Military Draft: Selected Readings on Conscription* (Stanford: Hoover Institution Press, 1982).

[8]Doug Bandow, "The Case against Conscription," *Journal of Contemporary Studies* 5:4 (Fall 1982), p. 46.

[9]Ibid.

[10]Mackubin T. Owens, "Libertarian Follies," *Journal of Contemporary Studies* 5:4 (Fall 1982), p. 60.

[11]See the President's Commission on an All-Volunteer Armed Force, *Report* (Washington: U.S. Government Printing Office, 1970), pp. 23–28. See also Milton Friedman, "Why Not a Voluntary Army?" in John O'Sullivan and Alan Meckler, eds., *The Draft and Its Enemies: A Documentary History* (Urbana: University of Illinois Press, 1974), pp. 253–263.

[12]Gary Hart, "Create a System of Universal National Service," *New York Times*, April 14, 1985, p. E-23.

Index